Retirement Hacking

How to earn more, spend more,
and have more in a long
and happy retirement

OR

How to live an affluent retirement lifestyle with
secure investments and reliable cash flow without
the risk and volatility of the stock market

Bob Zachmeier

Out of the Box Books
Tucson, Arizona

This publication contains the opinions, ideas, and personal experiences of its author. It is sold with the understanding that neither the author nor the publisher is engaged in rendering legal, tax, investment, insurance, financial, accounting, or other professional advice or services. If the reader requires such advice or services, a competent professional should be consulted. Relevant laws vary from state to state. The strategies outlined in this book may not be suitable for every individual, and are not guaranteed or warranted to produce any particular results. No warranty is made with respect to the accuracy or completeness of the information contained herein, and both the author and the publisher specifically disclaim responsibility for any liability, loss, or risk, personal or otherwise, which is incurred as a consequence, directly or indirectly, of the use and application of any of the contents of this book. Examples in this book assume a federal tax rate of 22% but your effective tax rate may be lower. Check with your CPA, tax professional, or financial planner for personalized investment advice.

Copyright © 2024 by Bob Zachmeier

All rights reserved, including the right of
reproduction in whole or in part in any form.

ISBN: 979-8-9902968-0-0

For information on other books by Bob Zachmeier,
visit the publisher's website at:
www.outoftheboxbooks.com

When it comes to books… think Out of the Box!

Out of the Box Books
P.O. Box 64878, Tucson, AZ 85728

For Camille

I was blessed to find an intelligent wife who is beautiful inside and out, has a strong work ethic, great business sense, creative ideas, and the follow-through to turn them into reality. As my friend, spouse, travel companion, and business partner we've accomplished a lot together. As we transition into retirement, I look forward to exploring the country and the world with the love of my life.

"My most brilliant achievement was my ability to be able to persuade my wife to marry me."
— Winston Churchill

TABLE OF CONTENTS

TABLE OF CONTENTS

TABLE OF CONTENTS

<u>Figures in This Book</u>

TABLE OF CONTENTS

ACKNOWLEDGEMENTS

I thank God for blessing me with the ability to attract amazing people into my life. I've prevailed through many challenges due to the love and support of family and friends.

I thank my wife, Camille, who spent many evenings and weekends alone while I've worked writing my books and NoteCarry software. Her hard work and attention to detail has enabled us to close more than 4,600 home sales. Camille is smart, fun, and an awesome partner in business and life.

I thank my parents who taught me to see things as they *could be* rather than as they are. Dad passed away in 1996 and Mom in 2019, but their *vision* and optimism are alive and well in me today. Mom was my business partner in a fireworks stand in my teens, a silent partner in many of our real estate deals, and the main proofreader of my first six books. This is my first without her editing, but my siblings, Mike, Becky, and Kathy, all stepped in to help, as well as Christian Hasselberg, Ken Collins, Tina Steel, and my wife, Camille.

I thank my brother, Mike, for bringing a unique and valuable perspective to our real estate business for 10 years. He got straight A's his entire life and always made me look bad, but his attention to detail has often come in handy! He also does an awesome job at catching mistakes in my books.

I thank my Scoutmaster, Val Heck, and all of the adult volunteers who donated hundreds of hours to help me earn the 36 merit badges required to become an Eagle Scout. My life is a collection of experiences made possible by generations of people who've given freely of their time, talents, and financial resources to benefit others. Their compassion for their fellow human beings sets an example for the rest of us to follow.

I thank Walter Wofford for his creative investment strategies and willingness to share his knowledge with others. If you look up *southern hospitality* in the dictionary, you're certain to find a photo of Walter and his beautiful wife, Laura.

I thank H. Quincy Long, CEO of Quest Trust Company, for using his unique skill set to teach others how to create a better retirement. Quincy is probably the only person in the country who is an experienced title company attorney, has owned a tax preparation franchise, founded an IRA custodial company, and understands creative investment strategies. He and his wife, Marsha, have a passion for helping people save.

I thank my business partner, Kelly Anne Porter, for her behind-the-scene efforts on our investment deals and the endless hours spent working in my booth at note conferences.

I thank Yolanda Estrada for helping me keep all the "balls in the air" on my local deals and her husband, Francisco Estrada, for his help to develop the *NoteCarry.com* website.

I thank the members of the NoteCarry Network who've placed their trust in me to teach them how to be note investors, and all the retirees who have partnered with me on note investments to create win-win-win deals in our communities.

INTRODUCTION

If you want to live like a millionaire but your net worth isn't $1,000,000, this book will help you.

A study conducted in 2023 by *Zippia.com* found that 8.8% of the adults in the United States have a seven-figure net worth and have earned the title of *millionaire*. If you're one of the 22 million Americans who've reached this financial milestone, congratulations! If not, this book can help you enjoy a better lifestyle than those who have more assets.

Being in the *two comma club* may be impressive on paper, but don't celebrate just yet! The value of your assets doesn't determine the lifestyle you'll be able to enjoy in retirement. The *income* from your assets determines how much you can spend after you've retired.

Let's assume that the millionaires followed conventional wisdom and paid off their home, cars, and all other debts prior to retiring. Following roughly the same ratios as an average American family, they would have 60% of their net worth in their home ($600,000) and two relatively new cars which *each* represent 5% of their net worth ($100,000). Their furniture, clothes, tools, equipment, etc. would represent 5% of their net worth, ($50,000), which leaves $250,000 of the $1,000,000 to be invested.

Let's further assume that since they have retired, they are not adding to their nest egg and thus must protect it by making secure investments which produce consistent returns without the risk of market volatility. If they earn a 7.00% return, the interest from the $250,000 they've invested would be $17,500 per year, or $1,458 per month.

That's not enough to pay the property tax on their $600,000 home in some states, and certainly not nearly enough to fund the extravagant millionaire lifestyle expected by anyone who watched the *Lifestyles of the Rich and Famous* television show!

If you're wondering why the millionaire's expendable income is so low in this example, it's because 75% of the $1 million they've accumulated is tied up in things that *cost* money, and only 25% is invested in things that *earn* money!

Many of our friends and real estate clients are struggling to live the retirement lifestyle they dreamed of having after a lifetime of work. The income that was once enough to live on five or ten years ago, no longer enables them to live comfortably. I decided to write this book after many conversations discussing these challenges and sharing the steps I've taken to avoid them.

It doesn't matter if you've already retired, are working toward retirement, or are just starting your first job. This book will enable you to save more, retire sooner, and enjoy a better lifestyle than many who have a higher net worth than you do. Enjoy!

1

Define Your "Dream" Retirement

"It takes as much energy to wish as it does to plan."
— *Eleanor Roosevelt*

Retirement is empowering. It's the one time in your life that you get a *re-do*, instead of playing the hand someone else dealt to you. This is your chance to reshuffle the deck, lay all the cards face up, and choose the hand you want to play for the rest of your life!

Throughout life, where you live is determined by your parents, your field of study, your job, the best school districts, etc. But at retirement, you can pack up your belongings and move anywhere on the planet! When you no longer trade your time for money, your employer can't dictate how much you'll be paid. For the first time in your life, *you* get to decide how much money you need to enjoy the lifestyle you choose.

Retirement isn't an *age*; it's a financial goal. When you reach it, you can quit your job and live on investment income! Unfortunately, few people plan well enough to enjoy the boundless freedom offered by retirement. During the first five decades of life, our time is consumed by attending school, building a career, raising a family, paying for college, planning weddings, and babysitting grandchildren. Then one day, you wake up in your fifties and realize, "Oh no, I forgot to save!"

We dream of retiring our entire lives, being able to do what we want, when we want, where we want, with whom we want, *if* we want. But we often can't plan for the ups, downs, curves, and distractions in our life. As a result, few people have the financial freedom to enjoy the lifestyle they dreamed of having in retirement. If your goal isn't quantified, written down, reviewed regularly, and given a deadline, it isn't a goal at all; it's just a dream that is unlikely to come true.

It's never too late to plan your retirement, even if you've already retired. This book contains several steps to help you plan for, or improve, your "Golden Years."

Step 1 - Estimate How Long You'll Live

In order to plan your retirement, you'll need to estimate how many years your money needs to last. Your family history can give you some clues, assuming that you'll live as long as your grandparents and parents, but the best estimate of how many years you're likely to live is found in the actuarial tables used by the Social Security Administration, which can be accessed at: https://www.ssa.gov/oact/STATS/table4c6.html.

If you haven't checked the life expectancy tables in a while, you may have longer to live than you think. Medical breakthroughs are helping people live longer, and the longer you live, the longer you're likely to continue living.

According to the Period Life Table published in the Social Security Administration's 2023 Trustees Report, at age 55, men are expected to live until they're 79.27 years old and women until they're 82.86 years old. But at age 65, both sexes gain two years; men are expected to live until they're 81.94 years old and women until they're 84.66 years old.

It's important to plan ahead so your income doesn't run out before you die. However, overestimating how long you will live reduces the amount you can spend each year, needlessly limiting the lifestyle you can enjoy.

Step 2 - Calculate How Much You Need To Live

Many people underestimate how much they'll need in retirement. They assume that since their home (their largest expense) will be paid off and they'll no longer be commuting to work, they won't need as much money as they did when they were working.

The problem with this theory is that while you're working, a significant portion of your time each day is spent getting ready for work, driving to work, working, and driving home. Aside from an hour off for a lunch break, you're not spending any money during the majority of each work day. When you retire, the hours previously dedicated toward working now offer new opportunities to spend money on things like golf, tennis, crafts, travel, or other new adventures. You're likely to spend *more* money when you retire, not less.

To calculate how much money you'll need each month, start with the amount you spend now. Write down the things you currently spend money on each month. Many people cringe at the idea of a budget because they associate budgets with giving up things they enjoy. It's actually the opposite when planning for your retirement.

Documenting how much money you'll need to enjoy the lifestyle you want is crucial in determining when you can retire. This is *not* the time to cut out expenses because you don't think you can afford them; it's the time to add them so you won't be short when you retire. You're likely to find things you no longer use or need. Getting rid of these wasteful expenditures will give you even more money to spend.

CHAPTER 1 – DEFINE YOUR "DREAM" RETIREMENT

Many people have only their jobs to provide the income they need to live. In Figure 1-1 and Figure 1-2, there are more than 100 monthly expenses that a typical family might incur. The expenses are divided into 12 categories and take up two pages of this book. No wonder so many people find it difficult to save for retirement!

Figure 1–1 Typical Monthly Expenses

HOUSING		ENTERTAINMENT	
Mortgage Principal		Vacation / Travel	
Mortgage Interest		Concerts / Games	
Property Tax		Date Night	
Hazard Insurance		Club Memberships	
HOA Dues		Education / Classes	
Pest Control		Hobby Supplies	
Lawn / Snow Removal		Movies / Books	
Landscaping		Newsletters / Magazines	
Maintenance		Cable TV	
Repairs		Other:	
Electric		**HOUSEHOLD**	
Gas		Furniture	
Water / Sewer		Furnishings	
Trash / Hauling		Towels / Linens	
Other:		Other:	
AUTOMOBILES		**COMMUNICATIONS**	
Car Payment		Cellular Phone	
Fuel / Fluids		Home Telephone	
Oil Changes / Tires		Internet Service	
Cleaning / Care		Postage	
Car Repairs		Other:	
Auto Insurance		**PETS**	
Auto Club Membership		Food	
Licensing Fees		Veterinary Care	
Parking		Medicine	
Tolls		Toys / Equipment	
Radio / Music Fees		Pet Sitting	
Other:		Other:	

Figure 1–2 Typical Monthly Expenses (continued)

HEALTH		FINANCIAL	
Doctors		Retirement Savings	
Dentists		Vehicle Replacement	
Prescription Drugs		Investments	
Gym / Trainers		IRA Contributions	
Yoga / Classes		Professional Fees	
Sports Leagues		Conferences / Classes	
Hair Care		Brokerage Fees	
Nails / Pedicures		Bank / Credit Card Fees	
Personal Hygene		Interest Fees	
Other:		Miscellaneous Cash	
FOOD		Emergency Fund	
Groceries		Other:	
Restaurants		**TAXES**	
Home Delivery Fees		Federal Income Tax	
Wine / Beer / Drinks		State Income Tax	
Food Clubs		City / County Tax	
Coffee / Beverages		Other:	
Snacks / Treats		**GIFTS**	
Vitamins / Supplements		Tithing	
Other:		Political Contributions	
CLOTHING		Birthday / Anniversary	
Clothes		College Tuition	
Shoes		Trust Funds	
Dry Cleaning		Holiday Decorations	
Other:		Other:	
		GRAND TOTAL	

Use your expense estimates above to create the lifestyle you'd like to afford in retirement. Don't hold back! Enter a realistic monthly amount for each item you'd like to include, even if you don't think you can afford it. In this exercise, you're creating your dream lifestyle with no boundaries. I'll help you find ways to afford that lifestyle as we go through the retirement planning process together.

2

Add Up Your Assets

"Money isn't everything, but it is when you start thinking about putting money away for your retirement days."
— Andre Leon Talley

In the last chapter, you determined how many years you're likely to live and how much the dream lifestyle you've planned will cost each month. The next step is to figure out where the money will come from to pay for your lifestyle. Financial terms are typically stated in years, not months, so if your dream lifestyle will require $10,000 per month, simply multiply the monthly cost by 12 to calculate the annual income you'll need ($10,000 x 12 = $120,000).

To calculate the total amount you'll need throughout retirement, multiply the income you'll need each year by the number of years you're likely to live. If the life expectancy tables predict that you'll live 20 years after you retire, then multiply your annual income requirement by 20 to find how much you'll spend in retirement. In this example, you'll need $2.4 million ($120,000 per year x 20 years = $2,400,000).

Don't be alarmed if the total you'll spend after retiring is much higher than the amount you currently have. In this example, the $2,400,000 is *not* the amount you'll need to start with at retirement; it's the total you'll receive over 20 years from Social Security, your pension, and investments.

When you're no longer receiving paychecks from your job, your monthly living expenses will be paid from Social Security, pension payments, Individual Retirement Accounts, 401(k) distributions, and your savings. To figure out how you'll pay for your retirement lifestyle, use the Net Worth Worksheet in Figure 2-1 to list all of the assets (and liabilities) you have. Include your home, cars, bank accounts, stocks, bonds, retirement accounts, cash, and any debts.

Figure 2-1 Net Worth Worksheet

REAL ESTATE	Value	Debt	Equity	Income
Primary Residence				
Vacation Home				
Rental Properties				
Land / Other				
Total Real Estate				
INVESTMENTS	Value	Debt	Equity	Income
Savings / Checking				
CDs / Money Market				
Stocks				
Bonds				
Mutual Funds				
Promissory Notes				
Jewelry / Art / Crypto				
Life Insurance / Other				
Total Investments				
RETIREMENT	Value	Debt	Equity	Income
Traditional IRA				
Roth IRA				
401(k) / 403(b)				
Roth 401(k) / 403(b)				
Health Savings Acct.				
Annuities / Other				
Total Retirement				
VEHICLES	Value	Debt	Equity	Income
Cars / Trucks / SUVs				
RV / Camper / Boat				
Motorcycles / Other				
Total Vehicles				
DEBTS	Value	Debt	Equity	Income
Credit Cards	$0			
Medical / Other Debt	$0			
Taxes Owed / Other	$0			
Total Debts	$0			
TOTAL ASSETS				

When the worksheet is complete, you'll have a comprehensive list of everything you own, its market value, and the amount of debt, if any, owed on each asset. By subtracting the debt in each row from the value, you can determine your net worth, the value of everything you own.

Most of the people I talk with about retirement know the value of the assets they own, but when I ask how much they're going to earn from those assets each month, I'm shocked by how many people don't know. As we learned from the "millionaires" in the Introduction, what you *own* isn't nearly as important as the income it produces. How can you retire if you don't know how much you'll earn?

To calculate how much income your assets generate, enter the annual income produced by each asset in the right-hand column of Figure 2-1. It's sobering for most people to realize that their largest physical "assets" (home and cars) don't produce any income, and actually produce *expenses* every month (insurance, taxes, maintenance, fuel, etc.).

This exercise can drastically change how rich or poor you feel. Those who retire with $500,000 in net worth could earn more monthly income than those with $2,000,000 in assets, depending on how well their assets are distributed and managed.

Your ability to retire isn't based upon your age or even how much money you've saved. You can retire at any age as long as the amount you *earn* is enough to offset the amount you *burn*. Those with a lower burn rate can retire much sooner.

3

Social Security Saves the Day!

"Today more people believe in UFOs than believe that Social Security will take care of their retirement."
—Scott Cook

Social Security is a controversial subject. Some believe it is the best thing our government ever accomplished for its citizens and others believe it's the biggest Ponzi scheme in history. The Old-Age, Survivors, and Disability Insurance (OASDI) program, commonly known as "Social Security," was part of President Franklin D. Roosevelt's post-depression New Deal program.

During the Great Depression, poverty rates among senior citizens exceeded 50 percent. The Social Security Act of 1935 was passed as "an attempt to limit unforeseen and unprepared-for dangers in modern life, including old age, disability, poverty, unemployment, and the burdens of widows and widowers with and without children."

In 1937, the first 20 million Social Security cards were issued and the government began deducting Federal Insurance Contributions Act (FICA) tax and Self-Employed Contributions Act (SECA) tax from workers' paychecks. On January 31, 1940, the first benefit check for $22.54 was issued to Ida May Fuller, a retired legal secretary from Ludlow, Vermont. At the time, most women weren't eligible to receive Social Security benefits because agricultural and domestic workers were excluded.

When the Social Security Act was passed in 1935, the average life expectancy was 60 years for men and 64 years for women. Ida May Fuller beat the odds, collecting more than 400 Social Security checks before dying in 1975 at the age of 100. The $22,888.92 Ms. Fuller received was 924 times more than she contributed. She retired three years after the program was introduced and outlived the actuarial tables by 36 years.

The amount recipients received each month didn't change for the first 10 years, but in 1950, a 77% Cost Of Living Adjustment (COLA) was added. During the next 25 years, COLAs were sporadic, requiring special legislative sessions, but they became mandatory in 1975. Since then, in the 3rd quarter of each year, the inflation indicated by the Consumer Price Index for Urban Wage Earners and Clerical Workers (CPI-W) becomes the COLA for Social Security in January of the following year. Figure 3-1 provides the history of cost of living adjustments since they became mandatory in 1975.

Figure 3-1 Social Security Cost Of Living Adjustments

Year	COLA	Year	COLA	Year	COLA
1975	8.0%	1992	3.7%	2009	5.8%
1976	6.4%	1993	3.0%	2010	0.0%
1977	5.9%	1994	2.6%	2011	0.0%
1978	6.5%	1995	2.8%	2012	3.6%
1979	9.9%	1996	2.6%	2013	1.7%
1980	14.3%	1997	2.9%	2014	1.5%
1981	11.2%	1998	2.1%	2015	1.7%
1982	7.4%	1999	1.3%	2016	0.0%
1983	3.5%	2000	2.5%	2017	0.3%
1984	3.5%	2001	3.5%	2018	2.0%
1985	3.5%	2002	2.6%	2019	2.8%
1986	3.1%	2003	1.4%	2020	1.6%
1987	1.3%	2004	2.1%	2021	1.3%
1988	4.2%	2005	2.7%	2022	5.9%
1989	4.0%	2006	4.1%	2023	8.7%
1990	4.7%	2007	3.3%	2024	3.2%
1991	5.4%	2008	2.3%	**AVG.**	**3.8%**

The 8.7% increase in 2023 was the largest since 1980 and 1981, the only other time inflation in the United States reached double digits since mandatory cost of living increases began in 1975. From 2003 to 2023, the COLA averaged 2.6%, but there were no increases in 2010, 2011, or 2016, which significantly lowers the average. Since annual adjustments began in 1975, the average Social Security COLA has been 3.8%. This is why many financial planners use 4% when planning for inflation.

The Social Security program has been expanded over time to include agricultural and domestic workers, disabled workers and their children, disabled adult children, and the dependents and surviving spouses of those who've died. According to the Social Security website, there were 71,725,000 beneficiaries receiving monthly payments in January 2024, and 12,000 more Americans are turning 65 every day.

There are tens of millions more people collecting Social Security benefits each month than were initially planned for and they're living a lot longer. New research published by the American Medical Association in November 2023, put the average life expectancy of American men at 73.2 years and women at 79.1 years. Men are living 13.2 years longer than they were in 1935 and women are living 15.1 years longer.

The cost of benefits has increased exponentially and so have the payroll taxes that fund them. When Social Security was first introduced, workers were taxed 2% on the first $3,000 earned each year. By 2024, the tax had increased to 12.4% of the first $168,600 earned, with an additional 2.9% tax for Medicare.

In addition to raising payroll taxes, the government also raised the "normal" retirement age from 65 to 67 and imposed a tax on the Social Security benefits paid to retirees who have income in addition to Social Security benefits. If your income plus *half* your Social Security benefit is over the *base amount*, you'll be taxed. In 2024, the base amount was $25,000 for single filers and $32,000 for those who file jointly.

In 2024, the average benefit payment to Social Security recipients was $1,907 per month. These payments account for 21% of the national budget. If you also consider that Medicare payments account for 24% of the budget, nearly half of what we spend as a nation goes to care for our aging population. Social Security is *not* an entitlement program; it's the return of the money taken from workers and held without interest for five decades. A debt is owed to the people who paid into the Social Security program and it needs to be honored.

Social Security is intended to *subsidize* your income, not be the sole source of it. But without it, 20 million more Americans would fall below the poverty line, unable to buy food, pay for utilities, or keep a roof over their head. Inflation has driven the cost of nearly everything higher, which is especially hard on those who live on a fixed income.

To set up a free online Social Security account, go to: www.ssa.gov/myaccount and click on Create an Account. You don't have to be at or nearing retirement age to create an account. Anyone who's paid taxes can open an account. The Social Security Administration will provide the history of how much you've paid in each year since starting your first job. If you're nearing retirement, you can find out how much you can expect to receive if you take early retirement at age 62, wait until "full retirement age" at 67, or "late retirement" between age 68 and 70.

The full or "normal" retirement age was 65 for many years, but in 1983, Congress passed a law to gradually raise the age because people are healthier and living longer. The law raised the full retirement age beginning with people born in 1938 and later. The age for "full retirement" increases by a few months for every birth year, until it reaches 67 for people born in 1960 and later.

Late retirement adds 8% to your benefit for each year that you wait to receive it after full retirement age. Some financial professionals call this a guaranteed return, but *life* is never guaranteed.

When you determine how much Social Security benefit you'll receive and add it to the income you're earning from your investments, you'll find the difference between your retirement income and the expenses required to live your dream lifestyle. We'll work on the shortfall (if any) later in the book. In the next chapter, we'll determine whether it's worth it to wait until full retirement age to start receiving your Social Security benefit.

4

Is It Worth It To Wait?

"Most decisions are not binary, and there are usually better answers waiting to be found if you do the analysis and involve the right people."
— Jamie Dimon

Many financial professionals recommend that you wait as long as possible to take your Social Security so you can collect a larger check, but you really need to calculate it for yourself to determine what's best for you.

Figure 4-1 shows an actual benefit estimate from the Social Security Administration that shows the three options this worker has to receive their Social Security benefits.

Figure 4-1 Social Security Options

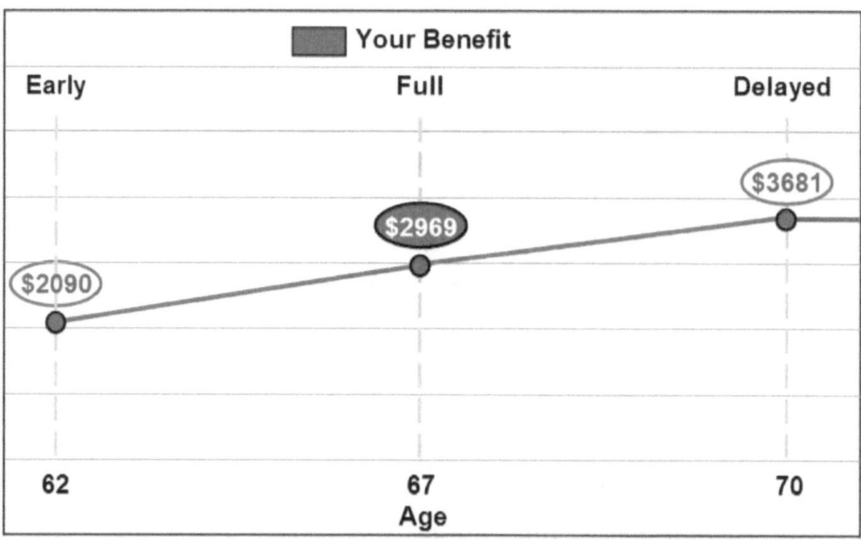

Option #1 - Start taking Social Security as early as possible at the age of 62 and receive $2,090 per month.

Option #2 - Wait until *full retirement age* to receive $2,969 per month ($879 more than option #1).

Option #3 - Wait until the age of 70 to receive $3,681 per month ($1,591 more than option #1).

CHAPTER 4 – IS IT WORTH IT TO WAIT?

In the situation presented in Figure 4-1, if you waited until age 67 to start receiving your benefit, you'd lose $2,090 per month for five years. Those 60 uncashed checks would total $125,400 plus the COLA increases each year for inflation. Getting an extra $879 per month may sound better, but it will take 12 years to recover the money you *didn't* take.

If you retire, but opt to wait for your Social Security check, you'll have to withdraw $25,080 each year from your investment portfolio ($2,090 x 12 = $25,080) to pay for your living expenses. If instead, you used your Social Security benefit to pay your expenses, the $25,080 would stay invested. At 7%, you'd earn $1,756 ($25,080 x .07 = $1,756), bringing your intact savings after the first year to $26,836 ($25,080 + $1,756 = $26,836). I'll share *how* to earn a predictable 7% return later.

In the second year, an additional $25,080 (plus COLA) would be withdrawn if you didn't receive Social Security to pay your bills. When added to the $26,836 "saved" in the first year you'd have $51,916, plus interest of $3,634 for a total of $55,550 after two years. The investment capital you don't withdraw continues compounding for five years while you're using Social Security checks to pay your bills.

In this example, if you wait until the full retirement age of 67 to receive the $879 higher check each month, you'll spend your investment capital and lose the interest on it for the rest of your life. If your capital wasn't withdrawn, it would grow to $154,325 plus whatever COLA increases are added over those five years. Figure 4-2 quantifies the capital preserved and the interest earned during the 5 years between age 62 and 67.

Figure 4-2 Accumulated Capital Over 5 Years

Age	Start of Year	# Checks Received	Total Received	7.00% Interest	End of Year
62	$0	12	$25,080	$1,756	$26,836
63	$26,836	12	$25,080	$3,634	$55,550
64	$55,550	12	$25,080	$5,644	$86,274
65	$86,274	12	$25,080	$7,795	$119,149
66	$119,149	12	$25,080	$10,096	**$154,325**

Even without COLAs, if your unspent $154,325 stayed invested at 7%, the account would produce $10,803 per year ($154,325 x .07 = $10,803) for the rest of your *life!* When you calculate how much that is per month ($10,803 / 12 = $900.23), you'll find that the return you'd receive on the money you didn't spend is higher than the $879 difference in benefit.

The beneficiaries who wait until 67 to collect will likely never catch up to the 62-year-old recipients because of the five year head start they receive. While the 67-year-old recipients were depleting their savings to live, the 62 year olds were growing theirs. The savings they accumulated will produce enough monthly income to offset their lower benefit check!

Even if you've paid into Social Security for decades, there's no guarantee that you'll receive benefits. Ephram Nestor immigrated to the United States from Bulgaria in 1913. After paying into Social Security for 19 years, he began drawing benefits in 1955. His benefits were terminated in 1956 when he was deported for having been a member of the Communist Party from 1933 to 1939. His wife remained in the United States but didn't receive his Social Security benefit.

Nestor sued the Department of Health, Education, and Welfare on the basis that he'd been deprived of his Social Security benefit without due process. In 1960, The Supreme Court ruled in *Flemming v. Nestor* that there is **no contractual right to receive Social Security payments**. Payments due under Social Security are not "property" and thus are not protected. The court upheld the constitutionality of Section 1104 of the Social Security Act in which Congress reserved the power to amend and revise the schedule of benefits.

Another reason to consider taking early payments is the long-term sustainability of the program. In March, 2023, the Social Security Board of Trustees projected that the Old-Age and Survivors Insurance Trust Fund and the Disability Insurance Trust Fund would run out of money in 2034. Both pay a portion of the benefits received by current recipients.

It's important to note that the Social Security Board of Trustees did NOT say that Social Security would be depleted in 2034. Their report said the *trust funds* would be depleted. If this should happen and Congress doesn't provide additional funding, the amount retirees receive would be reduced by approximately 20%. The majority of program funding comes from the payroll taxes of current workers, so as long as there are Americans working and paying taxes, Social Security will continue to pay benefits.

Since I began working in 1976, more than $400,000 was deducted from my paychecks to fund my retirement. I honestly thought that Social Security would be defunct before I became old enough to benefit from it. But, to my surprise, when I turned 62, it was still viable. I opted to take my benefit early. My father paid into Social Security for 35 years and received only *ten* payments before dying at the age of 62. My mother received a letter from the Social Security Administration explaining that since my father had not lived the last two days of October, she had to return the October check to them!

We received a similar letter when my mom died on September 27th and had to return the last payment. The Social Security Administration stopped paying in advance and now *floats* the payments by a month or more. The payments are held for a month before being transferred to your bank account during the week you were born. For instance, if you were born on November 15th, you'd receive your first benefit payment in the third week of December.

If you'll still be working at age 62, it doesn't make sense to take your Social Security early. There's a limit on how much you can earn if you collect before your full retirement age. In 2024, you could earn up to $22,320 without impacting Social Security benefits, but on any income over that, $1.00 is withheld from your benefit payment for every $2.00 that you earn.

In the calendar year in which you reach full retirement age, you can earn quite a bit more. In 2024, you could earn up to $59,520 before your Social Security benefit was affected. After you reach full retirement age, your Social Security benefits aren't affected, no matter how much you earn.

5

Inflation: the Income Assassin

"Inflation is when you pay fifteen dollars for the ten-dollar haircut you used to get for five dollars when you had hair."

— Sam Ewing

Inflation is the increase in the price of goods and services over time. When the price of something increases, it decreases the purchasing power of our money, thus reducing the amount we can buy. For example, if a can of soup costs $2.00, you could buy 5 cans for $10.00, but if the price increases to $2.50, the same $10.00 would buy only 4 cans of soup.

The price of fuel is one of the biggest drivers of inflation. Higher fuel costs increase the cost of raw materials because it costs more to operate the equipment to harvest the materials and ship them to factories. The factories that convert the raw materials into finished products are also affected by higher fuel prices, because it increases the cost to run their equipment and deliver the finished products to retail stores.

Retail stores are also affected because it costs more to run the equipment used to unload the finished products and heat or cool the building in which they are stored. When fuel prices increase, the cost of everything increases accordingly, and the added cost is passed on to consumers.

When employees have to pay higher prices for the things they purchase, they demand higher wages, which ultimately increases prices even more because employers must raise the price of the goods and services they offer in order to compensate their employees. This never-ending chain of events increases the cost of living every year.

Keeping inflation under control is the job of the Federal Open Market Committee (FOMC), which sets monetary policy in the Federal Reserve System. When demand is high and supply is low, prices tend to increase because there is not enough of a commodity to satisfy demand. The FOMC can decrease demand by raising interest rates, making money more expensive to borrow. Conversely, when demand is low and supply is high, prices typically decrease because there's more of a commodity available than people who want to buy it. The FOMC can increase demand by lowering interest rates, making money inexpensive to borrow.

Believing that some inflation is required in a healthy economy, the stated goal of the FOMC is to limit inflation to 2% per year. In other words, their goal is to turn every dollar you have this year into 98 cents next year! The FOMC hasn't succeeded at their goal of 2% inflation. In fact, the average rate of inflation in the United States from 1970 through 2023 is 4.04%, more than twice the goal set by the FOMC.

During the 54 years from 1970 to 2023, prices increased by 894.8%. An item that could be purchased in 1970 for $1.00 increased to $8.95 by the end of 2023. Figure 5-1 shows the rate of inflation in the United States each year since 1970 as reported by the Bureau of Labor Statistics. The right-hand column shows how much $100.00 in 1970 would buy at the end of each year. The U.S. dollar lost nearly 90% of its purchasing power in the 54 years between 1970 and 2023.

Inflation is especially important for retirees to consider. When you stop working, the money you've saved is all you'll have for the rest of your life. As inflation erodes the value of the dollar, it will require larger withdrawals from your savings each month to pay your bills.

Figure 5-1 Inflation in the United States 1970 – 2023

Year	Inflation Rate	Value of $100.00	Year	Inflation Rate	Value of $100.00
1970	5.84%	$94.16	2000	3.38%	$19.01
1971	4.29%	$90.12	2001	2.83%	$18.47
1972	3.27%	$87.17	2002	1.59%	$18.18
1973	6.18%	$81.79	2003	2.27%	$17.77
1974	11.05%	$72.75	2004	2.68%	$17.29
1975	9.14%	$66.10	2005	3.39%	$16.70
1976	5.74%	$62.31	2006	3.23%	$16.16
1977	6.50%	$58.26	2007	2.85%	$15.70
1978	7.63%	$53.81	2008	3.84%	$15.10
1979	11.25%	$47.76	2009	-0.36%	$15.16
1980	13.55%	$41.29	2010	1.64%	$14.91
1981	10.33%	$37.02	2011	3.16%	$14.44
1982	6.13%	$34.75	2012	2.07%	$14.14
1983	3.21%	$33.64	2013	1.46%	$13.93
1984	4.30%	$32.19	2014	1.62%	$13.70
1985	3.55%	$31.05	2015	0.12%	$13.69
1986	1.90%	$30.46	2016	1.26%	$13.52
1987	3.66%	$29.34	2017	2.13%	$13.23
1988	4.08%	$28.15	2018	2.44%	$12.91
1989	4.83%	$26.79	2019	1.81%	$12.67
1990	5.40%	$25.34	2020	1.23%	$12.52
1991	4.24%	$24.27	2021	4.70%	$11.93
1992	3.30%	$23.46	2022	8.00%	$10.97
1993	2.95%	$22.77	2023	4.10%	$10.52
1994	2.61%	$22.18	**Avg. Loss / Year**		**4.04%**
1995	2.81%	$21.55			
1996	2.93%	$20.92			
1997	2.34%	$20.43			
1998	1.55%	$20.12			
1999	2.19%	$19.68			

CHAPTER 5 – INFLATION: THE INCOME ASSASSIN

As mentioned in Chapter 3, the Social Security Administration added a cost-of-living increase in 1975 to help retirees combat the devastating impact of inflation. This increase covers only the portion of your income represented by Social Security. If you earn $5,000 per month and $2,500 of it comes from Social Security, the cost of living increase is on only 50% of your income. It's important to ensure that the other 50% of your income also has a cost-of-living increase built-in each year. I'll share how to do that later in the book.

Between January 2021, and December 2023, inflation drove prices higher, causing the spending power of the U.S. dollar to decline by 16.8%. In just three years, Americans were left with only 83.2 cents for every dollar they had in their bank accounts at the end of 2020. If your retirement plan didn't adjust for inflation, a $10,000 monthly spending allowance would have been reduced to $8,320 in just three years.

A loss of $1,680 per month would be hard for anyone to absorb, but those on a fixed income don't have the option of getting a raise or working overtime to compensate. Their only option is to withdraw working capital from their investments. When you withdraw money, the interest you earn decreases accordingly, so each time you subsidize your income by withdrawing investment capital, you're reducing your income for the rest of your life!

For the most recent information on the inflation rate in the United States, consult the U.S. Bureau of Labor Statistics (BLS) or the Federal Reserve. Both regularly release updated economic indicators and inflation data to keep you apprised.

RETIREMENT HACKING

6

Taking Out Taxes

"The problem is not that people are taxed too little, the problem is that government spends too much."
— *Ronald Reagan*

Income tax can take a huge bite out of your retirement savings, so it's important to know before you retire whether the money you've saved will be subject to income tax. The earnings in many employer-sponsored retirement plans haven't been taxed, but Roth IRA and Roth 401(k) accounts contain *after-tax* funds. Because the money in Roth accounts was taxed before it was contributed, no tax is due when the funds or the earnings are withdrawn.

Whether your retirement savings are taxable or non-taxable can make a huge difference on when you can retire. If the money has already been taxed, you may be able to quit your job ten years sooner than someone with the same amount that hasn't been taxed. Deducting income tax from each withdrawal affects the amount you'll receive and how long your savings will last. Figure 6-1 provides the income limits and corresponding tax for each IRS tax bracket in 2024.

Figure 6-1 IRS Income Tax Brackets for 2024

Income Tax Rate	Single Taxpayers		Married Taxpayers	
	Maximum Income	Maximum Tax	Maximum Income	Maximum Tax
10%	$11,600	$1,160	$23,200	$2,320
12%	$47,150	$5,658	$94,300	$11,316
22%	$100,525	$22,116	$201,050	$44,231
24%	$191,950	$46,068	$383,900	$92,136
32%	$243,725	$77,992	$487,450	$155,984
35%	$609,350	$213,273	$731,200	$255,920
37%	$609,350 or higher		$731,200 or higher	

Assume you've retired with $300,000 in an Individual Retirement Account (IRA). If you follow the advice often given by financial planners and withdraw 4% of the account's value in the first year, you'd take out $12,000 ($1,000 per month) to subsidize Social Security income ($300,000 x .04 = $12,000).

If the money in your account has already been taxed, you'll receive the entire $1,000 that is withdrawn each month. However, if the money in the account has *not* been taxed, you'll have to pay income tax on the withdrawal. If you're in the 22% tax bracket, $220 will be subtracted from your check each month for income tax, leaving you with $780 to spend instead of the $1,000 you originally withdrew.

If $780 isn't enough to pay your bills and you need to have $1,000, you'd have to withdraw $1,282.05 each month. After deducting income tax ($1,282.05 x .22 = $282.05), you'd have the $1,000 you need to pay your bills. Twelve monthly checks of $1,282.05 make your annual withdrawal $15,384.60 instead of $12,000. That's 5.128% of your account balance instead of the 4% you planned to withdraw. It may not seem like much, but it's 28.2% more each year. Larger withdrawals deplete your savings much faster, and it may not last as long as you need it to.

To ensure that you don't deplete your retirement savings too early, financial professionals often take the total you'll need for the year and multiply it by 25. To keep your spending allowance the same, pay the tax owed, and not exceed 4% of the total, you'd need to add another $84,615 to the $300,000 already saved. ($15,384.60 x 25 = $384,615).

The withdrawal schedule in Figure 6-2 assumes a starting value of $300,000 and a return of 7%. Your initial withdrawal will be 4% of the total with 4% added each year for inflation. In 35 years, you'd have $22,324 more than you started with after earning $906,150 and paying out $883,827.

Figure 6-2 Roth IRA Withdrawal Schedule

Account Value		% of Total	Return	Inflation
$300,000		4%	7%	4%
Year	Year Start	Paid Out	Interest	Year End
1	$300,000	$12,000	$20,160	$308,160
2	$308,160	$12,480	$20,698	$316,378
5	$332,918	$14,038	$22,322	$341,201
10	$373,855	$17,080	$24,974	$381,749
15	$411,105	$20,780	$27,323	$417,648
20	$438,816	$25,282	$28,947	$442,481
21	$442,481	$26,293	$29,133	$445,321
22	$445,321	$27,345	$29,258	$447,234
23	$447,234	$28,439	$29,316	$448,110
24	$448,110	$29,577	$29,297	$447,831
25	$447,831	$30,760	$29,195	$446,267
26	$446,267	$31,990	$28,999	$443,276
27	$443,276	$33,270	$28,700	$438,707
28	$438,707	$34,600	$28,287	$432,394
29	$432,394	$35,984	$27,749	$424,158
30	$424,158	$37,424	$27,071	$413,805
31	$413,805	$38,921	$26,242	$401,127
32	$401,127	$40,478	$25,245	$385,894
33	$385,894	$42,097	$24,066	$367,864
34	$367,864	$43,781	$22,686	$346,769
35	$346,769	$45,532	$21,087	$322,324
Total Paid Out:		$883,827	$906,150 in Interest	

The withdrawal schedule in Figure 6-3 assumes the same value of $300,000 and a return of 7%. The initial withdrawal will be 5.128% of the total (to pay the tax) with 4% added for inflation. The Traditional IRA would be depleted in the 28th year after earning $461,072 and paying out $768,701.

Figure 6-3 Traditional IRA Withdrawal Schedule

Account Value		% of Total	Return	Inflation
$300,000		5.128%	7%	4%
Year	Year Start	Paid Out	Interest	Year End
1	$300,000	$15,384	$19,923	$304,539
2	$304,539	$15,999	$20,198	$308,738
5	$315,907	$17,997	$20,854	$318,764
10	$323,748	$21,896	$21,130	$322,981
15	$308,893	$26,640	$19,758	$302,010
20	$256,604	$32,412	$15,693	$239,885
21	$239,885	$33,708	$14,432	$220,610
22	$220,610	$35,057	$12,989	$198,542
23	$198,542	$36,459	$11,346	$173,429
24	$173,429	$37,917	$9,486	$144,997
25	$144,997	$39,434	$7,389	$112,953
26	$112,953	$41,011	$5,036	$76,978
27	$76,978	$42,652	$2,403	$36,729
28	$36,729	$44,358	$0	$0
29	$0	$0	$0	$0
30	$0	$0	$0	$0
31	$0	$0	$0	$0
32	$0	$0	$0	$0
33	$0	$0	$0	$0
34	$0	$0	$0	$0
35	$0	$0	$0	$0
Total Paid Out:		$768,701	$461,072	in Interest

In Figure 6-2, the $300,000 in the retirement account had already been taxed. The 35 years of payouts would total $883,827 and there would still be $322,324 remaining. That's a total of $1,206,151. If you retired at 65 years old, you'd be 100 years old!

In Figure 6-3, the $300,000 in the account hadn't been taxed. Due to a larger withdrawal to pay the tax each year, the payouts would only last midway through the 28th year. The total paid out would be $768,701 with nothing remaining.

The difference between the two is *not* the 22% income tax rate, its $437,450, which is 145.85% more than the $300,000 you started with at retirement ($437,450 / $300,000 = 145.85%). Taxes paid after the balance has grown are much higher than if paid upfront when the balance is low. This is why many people are advised to rollover their retirement savings into tax-free accounts before retiring.

7

Get Rid of RMDs

"The IRS is like the Mafia, they can take anything they want!"
— Jerry Seinfeld

If you have untaxed retirement savings in a Traditional IRA, SEP IRA, SIMPLE IRA, 401(k), 403(b), or 457(b) account, it's important to know that there are age-based requirements that mandate when the funds must be withdrawn.

These accounts allow untaxed retirement savings to grow for decades, but at a certain age, the government wants to be paid. The Required Minimum Distribution (RMD) establishes a timeline to make minimum withdrawals from your account each year. When your retirement savings are withdrawn from your account, the tax-free earnings stop, and the money becomes taxable. The government's patience nets them taxes on what's hopefully a much larger amount than you initially deposited.

The age at which you must start withdrawing your money is based upon life expectancy tables. Because people are living longer, the government is increasing the age at which the RMD must be taken. Prior to 2019, the RMD starting age was 70-1/2 but the SECURE Act raised it to 72 and the SECURE Act 2.0 extended the age further to 75. Figure 7-1 shows the RMD transition from 70-1/2 to 75 years old by 2035.

Figure 7-1 Required Minimum Distribution Age

Taxpayer Date of Birth	RMD Age
Before July 1, 1949	70½
July 1, 1949 - December 31, 1950	72
January 1, 1951 - December 31, 1956	73
January 1, 1957 - December 31, 1959	74
January 1, 1960 or After	75

To determine when you must start withdrawing the untaxed funds in your account, use the table in Figure 7-1 to find your birthday and the corresponding withdrawal age. You have until April 1st of the year *after* your birthday to take the first RMD, but don't forget! The penalty for not distributing on time had been 50% of the amount that was supposed to be withdrawn, but in 2022, the SECURE Act 2.0 reduced the penalty to 25%.

If you miss the deadline and fail to take the distribution during the first year, you may be able to reduce the penalty from 25% to 10% by taking two years of distributions during the second year. However, two distributions in the same year could significantly increase your income tax liability. You may get by *without* a penalty if you catch and correct the error before the IRS notices and fines you. If you find yourself in this situation, consult your accountant about what to do.

To calculate how much you're required to withdraw each year, you'll need the latest version of the Uniform Lifetime Table, which can be found in Figure 7-2 or online at www.irs.gov. To use the table, simply find your age in the left-hand column and the Distribution Period in the right-hand column. If you were born in 1959, Figure 7-1 shows that your first RMD begins at age 74. If you find age 74 in Figure 7-2, you'll find that there are 25.5 distribution periods remaining. Take the balance in your account at the end of the previous year, and divide it by the distribution periods remaining. If you had $300,000 in your account at the end of the previous year, you'd divide the $300,000 balance by the 25.5 distribution periods remaining to determine how much to withdraw

($300,000 / 25.5 = $117,764.71). If you have more than one IRA, you'll need to calculate the RMD for each account separately.

Figure 7-2 Internal Revenue Service Uniform Lifetime Table

Table III
(Uniform Lifetime)

(For Use by:

- Unmarried Owners,
- Married Owners Whose Spouses Aren't More Than 10 Years Younger, and
- Married Owners Whose Spouses Aren't the Sole Beneficiaries of Their IRAs)

Age	Distribution Period	Age	Distribution Period
72	27.4	97	7.8
73	26.5	98	7.3
74	25.5	99	6.8
75	24.6	100	6.4
76	23.7	101	6.0
77	22.9	102	5.6
78	22.0	103	5.2
79	21.1	104	4.9
80	20.2	105	4.6
81	19.4	106	4.3
82	18.5	107	4.1
83	17.7	108	3.9
84	16.8	109	3.7
85	16.0	110	3.5
86	15.2	111	3.4
87	14.4	112	3.3
88	13.7	113	3.1
89	12.9	114	3.0
90	12.2	115	2.9
91	11.5	116	2.8
92	10.8	117	2.7
93	10.1	118	2.5
94	9.5	119	2.3
95	8.9	120 and over	2.0
96	8.4		

CHAPTER 7 – GETTING RID OF RMDs

The RMDs you're required to take each year are taxed as earned income, but taxes aren't your only worry. If the distributions are high enough, you could exceed the income limits for Social Security and Medicare. If that happens, it could reduce your benefit payments or cause them to be taxed. This is something you'll want to plan for so you won't be caught off guard.

RMDs and their potential impact on Social Security and Medicare benefits can be avoided by rolling over your taxable accounts into a Roth IRA before you take Social Security. It's painful to pay the income tax upfront, but could be worth it to protect your Social Security and Medicare benefits. The tax-free return on your investments for the rest of your life could easily surpass the taxes paid, depending upon how long you live. A financial professional can help you develop a plan that will take you where you want to go.

Another important change included in the SECURE Act 2.0 was the elimination of RMDs for other types of Roth plans starting in 2024. The tax-advantaged retirement accounts that no longer require RMDs are the Roth IRA, Roth 401(k), Roth 403(b) and Roth 457(b). These accounts can provide more flexibility as you age because you can take out the money when you *need* it, not when the government wants to be paid. All Roth accounts contain after-tax money that enables you to earn tax-free returns for the rest of your life. The funds held in these accounts should be the last that you spend because they can grow indefinitely and be withdrawn at any time after 59 ½ without any tax liability. Roth IRAs are discussed in the next chapter.

8

Roth to the Rescue!

"The only difference between death and taxes is that death doesn't get worse every time Congress meets."
— *Will Rogers*

The Roth IRA was introduced as part of the Taxpayer Relief Act of 1997. This tax-free retirement savings plan is named for its chief architect, Senator William Roth of Delaware, who had served in the military before embarking on a highly-productive political career. Roth served through the presidencies of Lyndon Johnson, Richard Nixon, Gerald Ford, Jimmy Carter, Ronald Reagan, George Bush, and Bill Clinton.

Senator Roth was a proponent of the people. He promoted home ownership and self-reliance for the masses in retirement. He was highly regarded for his fight against wasteful government spending. He led one of the most extensive investigations into the Internal Revenue Service ever conducted, disclosing widespread abuse. He co-authored the IRS Reform and Restructuring Act of 1998 and in 1999 he published *The Power to Destroy*, a book about how the Internal Revenue Service became so powerful.

The Roth IRA differs from other retirement plans because it allows after-tax contributions to grow indefinitely without further taxation or mandatory distributions. Roth IRAs expanded the types of investments you could make, giving people the flexibility to invest in things they understand, rather than placing their trust in the stock market.

Earnings can be withdrawn tax-free when the account owner turns 59 ½ and the account has been open for five years. Funds rolled over from non-Roth accounts can also be withdrawn penalty-free after five years. Because taxes are paid upfront, distributions don't increase your taxable income or impact your Social Security and Medicare benefits.

To reduce the impact on the federal budget, Roth IRAs were originally limited to contributions of just $2,000 per year with an additional "catch up" contribution available to those 50 or older. The contribution limit has increased several times since 1998, as illustrated by the history provided in Figure 8-1.

Figure 8-1 Roth IRA Contribution Limit History

Years	Under 50	Catch Up	Over 50
1998 - 2001	$2,000	$500	$2,500
2002 - 2004	$3,000	$500	$3,500
2005 - 2005	$4,000	$500	$4,500
2006 - 2007	$4,000	$1,000	$5,000
2008 - 2012	$5,000	$1,000	$6,000
2013 - 2018	$5,500	$1,000	$6,500
2019 - 2022	$6,000	$1,000	$7,000
2023 -	$6,500	$1,000	$7,500

If you were a farmer, would you rather pay tax on the seed or on the harvest? Withdrawals from Traditional IRA accounts are taxed at the *harvest*, after the account has had decades to multiply in value. This significantly increases your tax liability in the future. Pre-tax IRA contributions are popular because they're deductible; reducing the taxes owed in the year the contribution is made. You may have more money to spend at the time, but you'll pay dearly for it later!

When you retire and withdraw the money from your tax-deferred retirement accounts, you're taxed on a much higher value. Your tax rate is likely higher than it was decades earlier when your income was lower. Worst of all, the tax comes when you're on a fixed income and can't afford it.

Figure 8-2 shows the compounded value of $100,000 invested for 50 years with taxes taken out each year and Figure 8-3 shows the same $100,000 invested in a tax-free Roth IRA.

Figure 8-2 Non-IRA Savings After Tax

Amt. Invested		Rate	Tax Rate	After Tax
$100,000		7.00%	22.00%	5.46%
Year	Start	Interest	Tax	End
1	$100,000	$7,000	-$1,540	$105,460
2	$105,460	$7,382	-$1,624	$111,218
5	$123,695	$8,659	-$1,905	$130,448
10	$161,358	$11,295	-$2,485	$170,168
15	$210,489	$14,734	-$3,242	$221,981
20	$274,579	$19,221	-$4,229	$289,571
25	$358,184	$25,073	-$5,516	$377,741
30	$467,246	$32,707	-$7,196	$492,757
35	$609,515	$42,666	-$9,387	$642,794
40	$795,102	$55,657	-$12,245	$838,515
45	$1,037,198	$72,604	-$15,973	$1,093,829
50	$1,353,009	$94,711	-$20,836	**$1,426,883**

If you earn a 7% return, but fall into a 22% income tax bracket, the after-tax yield on your investment is only 5.46%. The taxable interest on your $100,000 investment in the first year is $7,000. If you're in the 22% tax bracket, $1,540 of the $7,000 profit is paid in income tax ($7,000 x .22 = $1,540) and you'd end the year with $105,460. The tax-free Roth IRA would earn the same $7,000 return, but end the year with $107,000.

The difference of $1,540 is only 1.44% of the total, but as each year goes by, the money paid in taxes reduces the interest you'll earn the next year. After the 10th year, the difference is $26,547, which represents 13.5% of the total, not 1.44%.

Figure 8-3 Retirement Savings Without Tax

Amt. Invested		Rate	Tax Rate	After Tax
$100,000		7.00%	0.00%	7.00%
Year	Start	Interest	Tax	End
1	$100,000	$7,000	$0	$107,000
2	$107,000	$7,490	$0	$114,490
5	$131,080	$9,176	$0	$140,255
10	$183,846	$12,869	$0	$196,715
15	$257,853	$18,050	$0	$275,903
20	$361,653	$25,316	$0	$386,968
25	$507,237	$35,507	$0	$542,743
30	$711,426	$49,800	$0	$761,226
35	$997,811	$69,847	$0	$1,067,658
40	$1,399,482	$97,964	$0	$1,497,446
45	$1,962,846	$137,399	$0	$2,100,245
50	$2,752,993	$192,710	$0	**$2,945,703**

Over 50 years, the $100,000 taxed each year grows to $1,426,883, but the un-taxed Roth account grows to $2,945,703. The difference is $1,518,820 or 51.56% of your account value!

After you've passed away and no longer need your Roth IRA, your heirs will inherit the account without probate. If the account holder died prior to December 20, 2019, whoever inherited the Roth IRA receives tax-free earnings over their lifetime and pays RMDs based on *their* life expectancy. The lifetime benefit is no longer available on accounts that were inherited after the SECURE Act was passed. No RMDs are required, but 10 years after the death of the account holder, the funds must be withdrawn and the account is closed.

If you've already retired and don't have a Roth, you can still contribute to a Roth IRA if you have *earned* income. If not, you can rollover funds from a traditional account (a rollover is the transfer from one account to another). There's no age limit on who can open a Roth IRA and you can contribute 100% of the income you earn up to the maximum contribution limit. If you turn your hobby into a business, you and your spouse can each contribute into a Roth IRA each year to increase your *tax-free* income as you deplete your taxable funds.

Contribution limits are much higher for taxable accounts than for tax-free accounts. For example, in 2024, the limit for Simplified Employee Pensions (SEP) and Solo 401(k)s increased to $69,000 or 25 % of your salary; whichever is less, but the Roth IRA limit was $7,000. It's wise to contribute as much as you possibly can to all your IRA accounts because *any amount* can be rolled over from your taxable IRA accounts into your tax-free Roth IRA. For example, if you have $280,000 in a Traditional IRA that will be taxed when you withdraw it, you can roll it over into your Roth IRA where it will grow tax-free. It would take *40 years* to deposit that much at $7,000 per year.

This "back door" contribution enables taxpayers to roll over Roth IRA, grow it tax-free for decades, and avoid the hassles of RMDs in the future. Funding your Traditional IRA and then rolling it over into a Roth IRA became allowable by the Tax Cuts and Jobs Act of 2017.

Taxes must be paid on the amount that was rolled over, but the long-term benefit is usually worth it. The downside would be if you die earlier than expected. The taxes paid upfront on the IRA funds rolled over could reduce the value of your estate, which might not have been taxable. This is a complex question that requires the advice of a competent financial professional. If you live in a state that has income tax, but plan to retire to a state that doesn't, it may be better to wait to roll over your funds until after you've moved to avoid paying tax in the state you left.

The Build Back Better Plan, introduced by Joe Biden in 2021, would have ended many of the benefits created by his Delaware colleague, William Roth. The bill would have eliminated "back door" Roth IRA contributions, imposed RMDs on Roth IRAs that grew to more than $10 million, and disallowed any new contributions to large Roth IRA accounts. The bill passed in the House by a vote of 220 to 213, but thankfully, was defeated in the Senate by *one vote!* If they tried to take it away once, they'll likely try again, so time may be running out to convert your Traditional IRAs into Roth IRAs.

Converting taxable IRA accounts into a Roth IRA when the market is low can create a huge tax savings. For example, if a stock usually trades at $100 per share but the value drops to

$75, the investment could be converted into a Roth IRA at $75 per share. From that point forward, any gain you realize would be tax-free, so if the price of the stock returned to or exceeded $100 per share, the profit of 33% or more wouldn't be taxed.

The income taxes saved by contributing to a pre-tax IRA become due when you rollover the funds to a Roth IRA. If you wait until January to complete the rollover, the tax won't need to be paid until April 15 of the following year. This floats the IRS for 15 months, giving you time to grow the money and save enough to pay the tax bill!

Even if you have to take out a mortgage on your home to pay income tax on a Roth rollover, the example in Figure 8-2 and Figure 8-3 shows that it could be well worth it. When you die, your spouse will continue to receive the tax-free earnings and withdrawals you enjoyed. When your spouse dies, the heirs to your estate will get another ten years of tax-free growth before the account is distributed tax-free and closed.

9

Hedge Your Health with HSAs

"Health is not valued till sickness comes."
– Thomas Fuller

Fidelity Investments, in its 2023 Retiree Health Care Cost Estimate, determined that retiring Americans can expect to spend $157,500 each ($315,000 per couple) on medical expenses in retirement. According to Fidelity, the cost of medical care has nearly doubled since 2002 when one could expect to spend $80,000 for health care in retirement.

Some financial professionals estimate that health-related expenses could consume 15% of your retirement income because Medicare doesn't cover long-term care, dental work, dentures, eye exams, glasses, hearing aids, cosmetic or elective surgeries, and a variety of other medical expenses you may incur as you age.

The Health Savings Account (HSA) was created by Congress in 2003 to incentivize Americans of all ages to save money for current and future medical needs. HSAs were intended to cover the costs incurred before meeting your health insurance deductible. If you're enrolled in a high deductible health plan, aren't claimed as a dependent on someone else's tax return, and aren't covered by the health plan of a spouse or parent, you may be eligible for an HSA. The definition a high deductible plan is set by the IRS each year, so check current limits.

HSAs have no minimum contribution, no limit on how long the funds must be invested, and no requirement to withdraw the contributions or earnings before you need them. If you don't use the amount you contribute each year, it rolls over to the next year indefinitely. There's also no time limit on when eligible expenses can be reimbursed. The funds in your

HSA can be left to grow and multiply tax free for decades before you withdraw them to reimburse yourself for qualified medical, dental, and vision expenses.

An HSA combines the income tax deductions of Traditional IRAs with the tax-free earnings and distributions of Roth IRAs. I consider this to be the most tangible benefit Congress has given to the American people. Contributions made to an HSA reduce your taxable income, thus reducing the income tax you owe. Health-related expenses that occur before the HSA is formally established are not eligible for reimbursement, so open your HSA as soon as possible to lower your taxes and start growing your tax-free nest egg.

HSA funds can be invested in a variety of alternative investments such as real estate, notes, options, or stocks, but you can't invest in life insurance contracts or collectibles such as art, coins, stamps, alcohol, or other tangible personal property. The earnings accrue tax-free, and there's no tax if the withdrawn funds are used to reimburse medical expenses for you, your spouse, or anyone claimed as a dependent on your taxes (even if they're not covered by your HSA plan).

The maximum contribution limits for individual and family HSAs are set by the IRS each year. Try hard to reach the limit. Those aged 55 and older (not 50 or older like Roth IRAs) can make an additional "catch up" contribution. To maximize your contribution (and lower your taxable income), when both spouses reach 55, open an HSA for each of you to be eligible for two "catch up" contributions instead of the one "catch up" contribution you receive for a family HSA.

You don't have to be an employer or spouse to contribute to the HSA of an eligible person. Anyone can contribute until the annual limit is reached, but only the contributions made by the account holder are tax deductible. You don't need to have a job to have an HSA. Unemployed and self-employed people can open them if they meet the eligibility requirements outlined earlier. If the account is funded all or in part by employer contributions, it still belongs to the employee and goes with them if they change jobs.

The advantage of having a high deductible health insurance policy is a much lower annual premium. The disadvantage comes when you need the insurance, but must pay the high deductible before the insurance co-payments begin. Small amounts deposited to your HSA from each paycheck can offset the high insurance deductible, especially when the invested funds are growing tax-free.

The account holder is responsible for keeping a record of the contributions and withdrawals, and saving the receipts for the medical expenses being reimbursed by your HSA. Your plan's custodian isn't tracking the bills for you. When you submit a reimbursement request for qualified expenses, the custodian will send the money, but you must maintain the records. At the end of the year you'll receive IRS Form 1099-SA to file with your income tax return.

When you turn 65 and start receiving Medicare benefits, you're no longer eligible to contribute to an HSA, but can continue to grow and use the tax-free funds in your HSA for qualified expenses not covered by Medicare. With untaxed earnings and delayed withdrawals, it's possible to grow your HSA into the *millions.*

If you determine that you won't need as much for medical care as you've saved in the account, the money can be withdrawn. However, if at any time, funds are withdrawn from the account but not used for qualified medical expenses, you'll have to pay income tax on the proceeds. This is no different than withdrawals from Traditional IRAs or 401(k)s because the funds contributed and profits earned have never been taxed. If the non-qualified withdrawal occurs before you turn 65, you'll have to pay a 20% penalty in addition to the income taxes due.

Insurance premiums are not considered a qualified medical expense unless you're 65 years old or older. Even then, Medicare Supplemental and Medigap premiums aren't eligible expenses for an HSA to pay.

When you or your spouse passes away, the remaining funds in the HSA are not lost. The plan can be transferred to a surviving spouse tax-free and they can continue to receive the tax-free earnings and tax-free withdrawals you had. When you die, anyone can inherit your HSA, but if it isn't the account holder's spouse, then the account will no longer be treated as an HSA.

The beneficiary will be taxed on the account's fair market value at the time of death, less any qualified medical expenses paid from the account on behalf of the decedent within one year of their death.

A list of HSA-eligible expenses is provided in Figure 9-1, but go online to: *https://hsastore.com/hsa-eligibility-list* to ensure you have the most current list.

Figure 9-1 Health Savings Account Eligible Expenses

Abortion	Insulin
Acid reducers	Lab fees
Acne treatment	Laxatives
Acupuncture	Lip treatment (cold/canker sore)
Allergy & sinus medications	Long-term-care premiums
Ambulance	Medical alert bracelets
Artificial limbs	Medical records fees
Birth control	Medicare premiums (65+)
Blood pressure monitors	Medicated shampoo/soap
Body scans	Nasal sprays
Breast pumps & supplies	Nursing care
Breast reconstruction (cancer)	Occupational therapy
Breathing strips	Oxygen related equipment
Crutches, canes & walkers	Pain relievers
Childbirth	Physical exams
Childbirth classes	Physical therapy
Chiropractic care	Prenatal vitamins
Contact lenses & supplies	Prescription medications
Cough, cold, & flu medications	Psychiatrist care
Dental care, braces & dentures	Psychologist care
Diabetes supplies	Skin creams & ointments
Diabetes education	Sleep aids
Eye exams/surgery/glasses/drops	Smoking-cessation
Feminine hygiene products	Speech therapy
First-aid kits	Sunscreen & exposure remedies
Flu shots	Surgery (non-elective)
Guide dogs/food/supplies & care	Teeth grinding guards
Hearing aids & batteries	Thermometers
Heartburn medications	Sterilization & reversal
Hospital expenses	Ultrasounds
Infertility treatment	Vaccines
Inpatient drug & alcohol treatment	Wheelchairs
Insect repellant & anti-itch creams	X-rays

10

Your New Money Mindset

"Many folks think they aren't good at earning money, when what they don't know is how to use it."
— Frank A. Clark

Every day your money isn't working, interest is lost forever. Figure 10-1 shows the compounded interest on $100,000 over 30 years. It's amazing how much $100,000 can turn into when invested at a continuous 7% yield, but what if your money is idle 10% of the time? It doesn't seem like a lot, but 10% of 30 years is 3 years of lost interest. The 7% interest rate would be reduced by 10% to 6.3%.

Figure 10-1 Cost of Not Being Invested 10% of the Time

Year	Working 100% of the Time			Not Working 10% of the Time		
	Starting Value	7.0% Interest	Ending Value	Starting Value	6.3% Interest	Ending Value
1	$100,000	$7,000	$107,000	$100,000	$6,300	$106,300
5	$131,080	$9,176	$140,255	$127,683	$8,044	$135,727
10	$183,846	$12,869	$196,715	$173,300	$10,918	$184,218
15	$257,853	$18,050	$275,903	$235,215	$14,819	$250,034
20	$361,653	$25,316	$386,968	$319,251	$20,113	$339,364
25	$507,237	$35,507	$542,743	$433,310	$27,299	$460,608
26	$542,743	$37,992	$580,735	$460,608	$29,018	$489,626
27	$580,735	$40,651	$621,387	$489,626	$30,846	$520,473
28	$621,387	$43,497	$664,884	$520,473	$32,790	$553,263
29	$664,884	$46,542	$711,426	$553,263	$34,856	$588,118
30	$711,426	$49,800	**$761,226**	$588,118	$37,051	**$625,170**
	Interest:	$661,226	661.2%	Interest:	$525,170	525.2%

The cost of not having your money invested for 36.5 days per year (10% of 365 days) is the difference between $761,226 and $625,170. At a 7% yield, the lost interest would total $136,056 over thirty years. Calculate how many family vacations, date nights, concerts, and beers could have been enjoyed if the money was working all the time. The 10% of idle time actually costs you 21.8% of the total due to compounding. It is important to keep all your money working all the time. Having *lazy money* is a retirement killer!

CHAPTER 10 – YOUR NEW MONEY MINDSET

You were probably taught by your parents, a teacher, or a mentor that if something *increases* in value it's an asset, and if it *decreases* in value, it's a liability. For example, your home is an asset, because it's likely to increase in value and your car is a liability because it's likely to decrease in value.

Retirement is the finish line of a lifelong race. When you quit your job, your focus changes from *growing* your money, to *preserving* it. Everything you own should be reassessed with a new definition of whether it's an asset or a liability. This can be accomplished by asking one simple question, "Does this item *produce* income or *consume* it?"

If the things you own produce income, they're an asset; if not, they're a liability. Even things that don't cost anything to own (like a canoe or a bowling ball) are still liabilities because to use them costs money and they're not *earning* anything sitting in the garage. Things that don't produce income actually cost you the opportunity to earn income. With taxes, inflation, and monthly withdrawals, you can't afford to have any lazy money. You worked hard to save the money to retire; now your money needs to work hard for you!

Without a job, your daily living expenses must come from your pension, Social Security, and retirement savings. If the amount you *burn* is more than you *earn*, you'll have to sell investments to pay your bills. When there's nothing left to sell, you'll be forced to live on your credit cards to survive. When your credit limits are reached, you'll be forced to get a job and work for the rest of your life to be able to buy food, clothing, and shelter.

This can be avoided by getting all your money working for you to earn a higher rate of return than the rate of inflation. You may be feeling that you'll have to work forever and may never be able to retire, but I was able to do it in 22 years using the strategies outlined below.

The 10X Rule – While working in the oil field in my early 20s, I received per diem pay to offset the cost of living in hotels and eating in restaurants while working away from home. Several co-workers and I would bunk together in a corner room at a budget motel and save $100.00 of our per diem pay each week. The savings later funded the down payments on several properties I purchased.

In the early 1980s, I often carried $1,000 or more in cash that I'd saved from my per diem pay. It would've been easy to blow it, but my mom taught me something when I was a child earning an allowance that forever changed my life. If I saved 10% of my income, in order to buy a $30 concert T-shirt, I'd have to earn $300. To take a $500 vacation, I've have to earn $5,000, and to buy a $20,000 car, I'd have to earn $200,000. To constantly remind myself of this fact, I wrote "10X" on several small Post-It® notes and stuck them on my money clip and credit cards. Mentally adding a zero to everything before I bought it kept me from spending frivolously, and I've continued to do it my entire life!

Using this approach to analyze your expenditures provides the opportunity to determine whether $5 is reasonable for a cup of coffee. Although it doesn't seem like a lot, $5 every day turns into $35 per week, $150 per month, and

$1,800 per year! If you're saving 10% of your income, you'd have to earn $18,000 to buy *coffee!*

The average American family doesn't save 10%. According to Statista, the average savings rate in the U.S. in January, 2024, was 3.8%. In order to spend $1,800 on coffee, an average family saving 3.8% of their income would have to earn $48,649 ($1,800 / .038 = $48,649). That's more than a lot of people earn all year! I've found that most people with financial problems don't actually need more money; they just need to do a better job of managing the money they already have!

Invest Your Raises – After graduating college and working for a year, I got my first pay raise and was told it was the highest anyone on my crew had received. When I called my parents to proudly share the news, my father was abrupt with me, asking why I needed the extra money. I defended my raise, relating how hard I'd worked and why I *deserved* the pay increase. Dad said, "I didn't ask why you deserve the money, I asked why you *need* it." He continued, "You lived last month without that money, so why do you need it next month?"

When I finally understood his question, I agreed that I didn't need it. Dad got what he wanted. He said, "Good! Contact the Human Resources Department and put 100% of that raise into a savings plan." At the time our company had just started offering 401(k) plans, so I did what my father told me. I signed up to deposit my entire raise into my 401(k) every paycheck and continued to do it for 22 years until I retired.

As I watched my 401(k) multiply, I shared what I was doing with many of my friends and coworkers and encouraged them to do the same. What I didn't know at the time is that one of the friends I shared Dad's advice with would later become my wife. I like to joke that Camille's 401(k) grew so much I had to marry her!

During the 22 years I worked without giving myself a raise, I always had a side business. I bought a moving truck with a friend and moved people on weekends, owned a printer repair company, a real estate coaching business, and a note investing business, all while working over 40 hours per week at my *real* job. I determined that since my side hustles were done during my personal time, any money earned in them would be spent on discretionary items, such as cars and vacations, which I otherwise couldn't afford.

I find it interesting that many of the people are more focused on the *amount* they've saved for retirement than how much income it will produce each month. The income you earn is far more important than how much you have saved.

In Chapter 2, you compiled a list of everything you own and established a value for each item. How much of your net worth is producing income and how much is *lazy money* that's producing no income, or worse, costing money each month? In the next chapter, I'll share a variety of strategies to close the gap between the lifestyle you want and the income you have. Let's try to get as much of your money as possible working so you can reach your retirement goals.

11

What If I Need More Money?

"Failure is simply the opportunity to begin again, this time more intelligently."
— Henry Ford

If you don't have enough income to pay for the lifestyle you've chosen, you'll have to find ways to overcome the shortfall. When you start drawing from investments to pay bills, you don't just lose the investment capital you've withdrawn; you also lose the *income* it's producing. You'll have even less income the next month, requiring an even larger withdrawal in addition to the planned increases for inflation.

For example, if your income is $5,000 per month, but you need $5,500 to live, you'd be $500 short each month. Over the course of the year, you'll have to withdraw $6,000 from your investment account ($500 x 12 months = $6,000). If the account contains pre-tax money, when you cash it out you'll have to also pay Federal and State income tax (unless you live in Alaska, Florida, Nevada, South Dakota, Tennessee, Texas, or Wyoming which don't have state income tax).

If your Federal income tax rate is 22% and State income tax rate is 3%, you'd have to withdraw $8,000 to pay the 25% tax ($8,000 x .25 = $2,000) and still have the $6,000 that you need. If your investments return an average of 7% each year, withdrawing the extra $8,000 reduces your income by $560 every year ($8,000 x .07 = $560), which is $46.67 per month. Even if your expenses stay the same, the $500 per month shortage this year will increase to $546.67 per month next year.

The deficit will become worse every year until you run out of money and become insolvent. This is why it's so important to have a written retirement plan that takes into account your age, how long your money needs to last, and an annual cost of living increase (typically 4%) for inflation.

CHAPTER 11 – WHAT IF I NEED MORE MONEY?

If unanticipated expenses or lower than expected income leave you with a budget shortfall, it must be dealt with immediately before the situation spirals out of control. You can resolve a deficit by earning more, spending less, or both. A variety of solutions are provided below.

EARN MORE

Work Longer – Working longer enables you to keep adding to your retirement savings before you start withdrawing them. If you work for an extra year, invest $1,000 per month in your Roth IRA and HSA, and don't tap your savings, the $1,000 saved and the $5,000 not withdrawn from your retirement savings would total $6,000 per month and $72,000 for the year. If you earned a 7% return on the additional savings, that extra year of work would produce $5,040 every year ($420 per month) for the rest of your life.

Monetize Your Hobby – Turning your hobby into a business can provide additional income that can be invested in your HSA (if you're not on Medicare) and Roth IRA. You also may be able to deduct a portion of your home, vehicle, and travel expenses, which will reduce your income tax burden.

Earn a Better Return – It's important to monitor the rate of return you're earning on your investments. There may be other investments that pay a higher return or have lower management fees. Although risk and reward usually go hand in hand, I'll discuss investments which can lower your risk, increase your yield, and don't have any management fees in Chapters 16 through 19.

Put Your Lazy Money to Work – Those who keep all of their money working to produce consistent income can enjoy a much better lifestyle than those who have only a small percentage of their assets earning income. You need to get the most out of every dollar by keeping them working full time. *Lazy money* can steal the retirement lifestyle you worked your entire life to enjoy! Lost income is lost forever!

SPEND LESS

Stop Automatic Payments – If you're struggling to make ends meet, contact your credit card company and report that your card has been compromised. It likely *has* been compromised by the companies billing it every month whether you use their services or not. Getting a new credit card gives you the opportunity to reevaluate whether you need that gym membership, book club, video service, or newsletter that's automatically paid for every month whether you use it or not.

Contact Service Providers – Recurring bills have a way of creeping higher over time. In the highly competitive Internet, cable, phone, and trash collection businesses, customer retention is crucial and they'll do a lot to keep you. Contacting these service providers to cancel your service will typically result in them lowering your monthly bill. We recently cut 50% off our cable bill and 40% off our cellular phone bill by making a phone call to cancel our service. Even though water, sewer, gas, and electric companies have no competition, they'll sometimes offer reduced rates to senior citizens who ask for a discount.

CHAPTER 11 – WHAT IF I NEED MORE MONEY?

Downsize or Move – You can save a lot on insurance, property tax, utilities, and maintenance by living in a smaller, less expensive home. If you're moving, why not choose a city or state with lower taxes, insurance, and cost of living?

Volunteer – Working as a retiree has benefits that aren't just financial. Many retirees find jobs or become volunteers for the social interaction that they don't get sitting at home. Helping others who have less makes you feel fortunate, and when you feel fortunate, you tend to be happy and grateful. It's also an inexpensive way to occupy your time, avoid spending due to boredom, and help others who need it.

Time Your Purchases – Many of the things we buy have selling cycles. For example, before Christmas, retailers charge full price for gift wrap, ribbons, decorations, and trees. But on December 26th, demand for these items wanes and prices are usually slashed 50% or more the day after the holiday. When the selling season is over, retailers gladly sell remaining inventory at cost or even at a loss to free up capital to purchase things that *will* sell. If their capital is invested in Christmas inventory, they'll lose the ability to double their money on all the other holidays. Seasonal clothing is another item with huge markdowns in the off season if you watch for sales.

Cut Off Your Kids –Retirement is your time to travel, visit old friends, and live life to the fullest! This is *your* retirement, not your children's. You can leave what's left for your children when you no longer need it. Giving a large amount of money to children who've never learned to save or manage their own funds is like handing the key to a Ferrari to a 5-year-old. Without discipline, they're likely to deplete your life savings in a matter of months. Enabling your children to live beyond their means is setting them up for failure after you're gone. They'll have a difficult time living on their income after you and your money are gone.

All of the topics covered in this chapter will get you closer to the retirement lifestyle you defined in Chapter 2. When people have a budget shortfall, they often think they need more money, but more income means more income tax and Social Security deductions. You'll also have to spend more on fuel and clothing.

When you cut expenses, you get to keep 100% of every dollar saved. Remember to add a zero to every expenditure to remind yourself that you must earn 10 times more to pay the bill. It's amazing how little daily purchases can turn into huge monthly and yearly bills. Remind yourself what you're working for:

If you do the things that others *won't*,
You'll have the lifestyle others *don't*.

12

Leveraging
Lazy Money

"The man who has no money is poor,
but one who has nothing but money is poorer.
He only is rich who can enjoy without owning."
– Orison Swett Marden

Movie stars who own homes all over the world often make headlines, but I can tell you from experience that having more than one home isn't the least bit practical. Camille and I purchased a second home in the White Mountains of Arizona in 2010 at the bottom of the Great Recession. The 3-bedroom, 2-bath home had a two-car garage and was situated in a small gated community on a golf course.

The home was 180 miles from our home in Tucson, but at 6,300 ft. elevation, it was often 30 degrees cooler during the summer months. Our neighbors had paid more than twice as much for their homes four years earlier, but during the worst housing market since the Great Depression, we purchased ours for 45% of the price it had been previously sold for when new.

During economic downturns, those who own two homes may have to decide which one to keep. Most people will choose to keep their primary residence and sell their vacation home. For this reason, home prices are more adversely affected during recessions in vacation areas than in areas with year-round residents.

During the first year of owning our second home, we made the 180-mile trip every other weekend to enjoy the cool mountain weather. We kept our Harley Davidson motorcycles in the garage and rode them more than 2,500 miles that summer, marveling at the sparsely populated areas with beautiful scenery, lakes, and pine trees everywhere.

When the real estate market rebounded, we got busy and each year, the visits to our mountain retreat declined steadily. When we did visit, it was often more out of obligation to check on our home because we hadn't been there in several months. We'd often arrive to find a violation from the homeowners association taped on the door for weeds or grass that was too tall. The fun weekend with friends in the mountains turned into sore muscles from hours pulling weeds!

The last two years we owned our mountain home, we visited only three times, but paid the expenses for the whole year. I told Camille that I thought it was time to sell, but she liked the idea of having a mountain escape during the hot Tucson summers and didn't want to sell our second home.

I explained that we were spending $10,000 each year for property tax, insurance, homeowners association dues, and utilities. By using our home only three weekends per year, each of the trips to pull weeds had actually cost us $3,333. That and the fact that within a few years the home would need a new roof, air conditioner, and exterior paint totaling $20,000 was enough to convince her to sell.

We sold the home, avoiding the future repair liability, and invested the equity in real estate notes, which I'll explain in Chapters 16-19. The $10,000 annual mountain retreat expenses were replaced with an income of $30,000 per year! The avoided expense and additional income from notes have added $40,000 to our budget every year since 2016. We've enjoyed vacations all over the world since selling our vacation home and we haven't pulled weeds at any of the destinations we've visited.

RETIREMENT HACKING

The value of our former home has appreciated since we sold it, but not as much as the income received from investing the equity. Since selling the home in 2016, we've avoided over $100,000 in property tax, insurance, utilities, HOA dues, repairs, and maintenance while earning $240,000 in income from the equity. The combined savings and income is nearly twice as much as we paid for the home!

Since purchasing my first rental property in 1982, I've wanted to own everything I could afford to buy, but after this experience, I no longer want to own anything other than our primary residence! Why pay all the expenses for a year if you are only going to use a property for a few weeks or even a few months? It makes more sense to keep your money working year-round and rent someone else's property. You pay for only the days you use, you won't feel obligated to go, and you will never have to be responsible for any maintenance.

Assume that you found a vacation home for $400,000 and have a $400,000 investment portfolio earning 7% interest. If you sold the investments, you could purchase the vacation home and have no mortgage. The idea of owning a vacation home may seem appealing until you add up the costs.

If the property tax is $4,000, insurance is $1,200, maintenance and repairs are $2,400 and utilities are $2,000, the expenses would total $9,600. Why would you trade $28,000 in income ($400,000 x.07 = $28,000) each year for $9,600.00 in *expenses?* The lost income and added expenses would reduce your expendable cash by $37,600.00 the first year and more each year after that as the invested funds compounded.

The home will likely increase in value over time, but to break even, it would need to appreciate by nearly 10% every year to offset the expenses and lost income. Unless you're planning to live in the home six months out of the year, it would make more sense to rent someone else's property to avoid the maintenance, utilities, tax, and insurance expense while your money is invested and earning interest.

The same principle can be applied to boats, planes, motorcycles, four-wheelers, and other toys that won't be used as often as you think. These things all require fuel, licensing, insurance, maintenance, and repairs to operate, and if that's not bad enough, they depreciate in value. The biggest cost of ownership is the lost opportunity to earn interest for the rest of your life on the money spent to purchase these toys.

When I was younger, I lived on a lake and owned several boats. BOAT is an acronym. Every time you use a boat, you should be prepared to Bust Out Another Thousand (BOAT) for fuel, repairs, storage, licensing, water skis, ropes, life jackets, etc. I also owned two used Corvettes. I got good deals on them, but the tires are soft and only last about 20,000 miles. I calculated that each time I filled the tank with gas, I'd spent the same amount on tire wear. I got the thrill out of my system within a year and sold the cars before they depreciated below the amount I'd paid for them.

My thought on owning the things Robert Kiyosaki calls "doodads" is *pay by the day, then walk away!*

72

13

Does Your Vehicle Add Value?

"Everything in life is somewhere else, and you get there in a car."
– E. B. White

The vehicle you drive is one of the most expensive things many people own, second only to their home, if they own one. After more than 100 years, America's love affair with the automobile is alive and well. Early in life, cars represent a huge portion of our net worth, but by the time the average person retires, their vehicle represents about five percent of their net worth and consumes about 10% of their monthly income.

Some associate expensive cars with success and spend more than 10% of their income to project the appearance of wealth. This practice is especially prevalent in young, single males attempting to attract a mate. I can tell you from experience that this strategy will backfire, because the people attracted by your money will be *spenders*, not savers. You'll be destined for a life of debt, continually paying interest on the things that you can't afford and shouldn't have purchased, leaving you unable to save or retire.

Even though they're a major expense, cars are rarely considered investments because they're likely to depreciate in value, especially sports cars. Unless you live in an urban neighborhood where the things you need are all within walking distance, you need a car to get to work, run errands, and get from one place to another.

Many retirees celebrate their retirement by purchasing new cars for themselves and their spouse. They rationalize the purchases with the belief that newer cars will be more reliable, won't require expensive repairs, and will last for the rest of their lives. Besides, it's nice having a new vehicle that is comfortable to drive.

Spending your lifetime vehicle budget upfront may not be wise. With advances in medical science, you could outlive the useful life of your car. Figure 13-1 shows the difference between buying a $50,000 vehicle and investing over 10 years.

Figure 13-1 – Opportunity Cost of Vehicles Over 10 Years

Year	Spent On Vehicle			Invested For Growth		
	Depreciation		Value	Appreciation		Value
0	%	Loss	$50,000	%	Gain	$50,000
1	26.0%	$13,000	$37,000	7%	$3,500	$53,500
2	15.6%	$5,772	$31,228	7%	$3,745	$57,245
3	15.6%	$4,872	$26,356	7%	$4,007	$61,252
4	15.6%	$4,112	$22,245	7%	$4,288	$65,540
5	15.6%	$3,470	$18,775	7%	$4,588	$70,128
6	15.6%	$2,929	$15,846	7%	$4,909	$75,037
7	15.6%	$2,472	$13,374	7%	$5,253	$80,289
8	15.6%	$2,086	$11,288	7%	$5,620	$85,909
9	15.6%	$1,761	$9,527	7%	$6,014	$91,923
10	15.6%	$1,486	$8,041	7%	$6,435	$98,358

According to *WallStreetMojo.com*, vehicles will likely depreciate in value by 26% in the first year and 15.6% per year after that. In the first three years of ownership, the depreciation on a $50,000 vehicle will likely be $13,000, $5,772, and $4,872 respectively, for a total loss of $23,644. During the second three-year period, the depreciation is much lower at $4,112, $3,470, and $2,929 respectively for a total of $10,511. The difference between the first three years and the second three years is $13,133. A brand-new vehicle will likely depreciate 55% more in the three years after purchase than the same make and model that is three years older.

Instead of buying two new cars for $50,000 or more each, why not buy two 3-year-old cars for $25,000 each and invest the $50,000 savings? At 7.00% interest, your $50,000 investment will produce $11,252 over the next three years. During that time, your $50,000 savings are accumulating interest and the new cars you didn't purchase will depreciate by nearly half their value.

Assuming the depreciation estimated in Figure 13-1, you could sell one of your 6-year-old cars for $15,846. If you added the $11,252 earned in interest, you would have $27,098, to buy the same model year you originally wanted to purchase. After three years of depreciation, the value of that $50,000 car would be $26,356, leaving a surplus of $742 to invest.

Three years later, the $50,000 initially invested will have produced another $11,252 in interest. You could sell your older vehicle, which after nine years would be valued at $9,527. When added to the $11,252 interest and the $742 surplus from upgrading the 1st car, you'd have $21,521, which is nearly enough to purchase a 4-year-old car; two years *newer* than the new car you originally wanted to purchase!

Over 30 years, you would be able to replace both cars *five times* with newer, more reliable models, while most likely avoiding expensive engine or transmission repairs. Instead of having two 30-year-old vehicles, your cars would be much newer and more valuable than those you initially planned to purchase brand new. You would also still have the $50,000 savings producing $3,500 or more in interest each year!

Spending 10% of your net worth on vehicles which will lose half their value in the first three years is expensive, but not nearly as costly as losing the income on that money for the rest of your life! Vehicles are far more reliable than they once were and can often last 200,000 miles or more. According to *USA Today,* the average motor vehicle on the road in the United States in 2023 was 12 years old. Another thing to consider is that older vehicles are much less expensive to insure and license than newer models.

Since 2001, I've driven three vehicles and none were purchased new. We recently upgraded the Jeep we tow behind our motor home for day trips to national parks, baseball stadiums, and other attractions. We were shocked to find the average price of 6-year old Jeep Wranglers with 80,000 miles was more than $30,000.

Instead, we found a much newer Jeep with only 7,500 miles. The owner had decided to purchase a Tesla after only nine months of ownership and sold the Jeep to us for $16,000 less than she'd paid for it! We saved another $4,000 because there's no tax on vehicles in Arizona if you buy them from an individual rather than a dealership.

For this reason, we purchase all of our vehicles online, searching nationwide, so we have a much larger selection to choose from. We can usually find low mileage, garage-kept vehicles in the color we desire. Most have been purchased out-of-state and we either flew one way and drove them home or drove both ways to get them.

Camille found her car in California. The vehicle was less than a year old and had been driven only 5,200 miles. We found the same car, one year newer, at a local dealership for $40,000, but we bought the used car for only $24,500 and paid no sales tax. Our one-way rental car happened to be the same make and model as the car we were driving to purchase, so we drove to California in a black car and returned in a white one after a long weekend in the wine country with our dogs.

Instead of the stressful interactions with high-pressure salesmen who confiscate your car keys for hours, we prefer to deal directly with the original owners who've owned and cared for the vehicles since buying them new. We've met many nice people, gotten far better deals, avoided tens of thousands in sales tax, and enjoyed mini-vacations on the way home.

I'm sure you can find used car horror stories from people who had nothing but trouble, but we've never had an issue with any of the cars we've purchased directly from the owners. Over the past 40 years, I've saved over $250,000 using this strategy to buy vehicles. The savings have been invested and growing for decades. Buying used cars is one of the biggest life-changing decisions I've ever made.

Unfortunately, many people buy vehicles they can't afford, finance them, and pay interest on the depreciating value. Within a few months of finally paying them off, they trade for a brand-new car and start the cycle all over again! Contrary to popular belief, you are *not* what you drive. If you have friends who judge you by the vehicle you drive, you should find new friends!

14

Does Owning Your Home Help?

"The home should be the treasure chest of living."
– Le Corbusier

RETIREMENT HACKING

Your home is an amazing asset when you're *working* and have decades for its value to appreciate, but when you've retired, you no longer have the time to wait for appreciation. You need income every month to pay your bills.

The value of your home will likely increase over time, but it won't pay any of your expenses this month, and in fact, *creates* a lot of them (property tax, insurance, HOA dues, utilities, repairs, and maintenance). When viewed in this new light, your largest asset is suddenly transformed into your largest liability!

According to the National Association of Homebuilders, home equity accounts for 62% of an average American family's net worth at retirement. For most people, housing is their largest expense, but it typically represents only 25% to 35% of their gross income, so how can it be 62% of their net worth?

Home equity usually isn't the result of making extra payments or being a disciplined saver. In fact, your mortgage statement arrives in the form of a bill every month. So how does this *expense* turn into an asset that accounts for nearly two-thirds of everything you've saved in your entire life?

Appreciation often represents the largest portion of a homeowner's equity because of the leverage created when a home is purchased with a loan. If you purchase a $300,000 home with a 5% down payment, you will pay $15,000 ($300,000 x .05 = $15,000) and acquire a loan for the remaining $285,000. Even though you invest only 5% of the home's value, you'll receive 100% of future appreciation.

If during the first year, the value of your home increases by 5%, your $300,000 home would be worth $315,000. The $15,000 increase in value represents a 100% profit on the $15,000 invested as a down payment when you purchased the home. This continues year after year for decades until the mortgage is paid off. Home values don't appreciate every year, but the cost to build them does. Over the life of your loan the value is likely more than double as the mortgage is paid off.

By the time you're ready to retire, your home will likely be worth $600,000 or more with no mortgage. That's *forty* times more than the $15,000 initially invested to buy the home, but there's a downside. You lose the *leverage* that created the majority of your wealth! When your mortgage is paid off, the 5% appreciation that once provided a 100% return now provides only a 5% return, which may not be enough to offset inflation. Which is smarter; the homeowner with a mortgage earning 100% on their leveraged home or the homeowner with no mortgage earning 5% on their home equity?

It's comforting to have your home paid off, with no debt and a large bank balance. Believe me, I get it. I'm married to someone who wants exactly that, but if your income isn't enough to offset inflation, taxes, and the ever-increasing cost of living, retirement may be short-lived for you!

Many have been taught that debt is *bad* and thus, should be repaid as quickly as possible. Although this is generally true for depreciating assets, such as cars, it's not true with appreciating assets, as illustrated by the leveraged home where the down payment increased in value by a factor of *forty*.

The value of your home is the same whether you have a mortgage or not. Home equity cannot be spent. It remains in your home until you either refinance or sell. Until that time, the "dead equity" earns you nothing! I jokingly tell people they'd be better off burying their money in a *hole* than paying off their home because a hole doesn't have property tax, insurance, HOA, or maintenance expenses!

Home prices have increased steadily for centuries with few exceptions. Below are the 5 main reasons homes account for nearly two-thirds of an average American's net worth at retirement:

Leverage – When people buy their first home, it's common to have a low down payment. If the home appreciates in value, 100% of the gain goes to the homeowner, even though they put 5% or less down. By the time they've retired, many Americans have paid off their mortgage.

Principal Pay Down – Each month, your mortgage payment feels like a bill, but part of the payment goes toward principal, reducing the amount you owe. The payment comes out of your checking account, but unlike rent, some of it comes back into your net worth as home equity.

Demand – The need for housing has never been higher. People are living longer, waiting longer to marry, and divorcing more often, creating a need for more homes. An already short housing supply was depleted even further by companies like Airbnb (Airbed & Breakfast) and VRBO (Vacation Rentals By Owner).

Homes that were once available for sale or rent are now functioning as *hotels*. The number of short-term rentals in the United States is estimated to be between 1.5 and 2 million.

Inflation – Homeowners borrow money at today's value and pay it back over several decades with money that's worth far less due to inflation.

Appreciation – Many of the things we purchase (food, utilities, gasoline, insurance, etc.) have no value after they're used, but homes can be used for decades and multiply in value. The materials required to build a home increase over time due to inflation. Home prices according to Federal Reserve Economic Data (www.FRED.gov) are provided for each quarter in Figure 14-1. Between January 1980, and January 2024, the median sales price of a home in the United States increased by an average of 4.3% per year.

During this 45-year period, major corrections occurred *twice*. The first was to correct unsustainable appreciation which occurred due to reduced lending standards leading up to the 2008 housing collapse. The second corrected the unsustainable appreciation that occurred due to ultra-low interest rates during the 2020-2021 corona virus epidemic. Both corrections followed huge increases in home prices that were brought on by the lending practices of banks.

If you had a loan for 80% of your home's value during this time, the return on your investment would have been 21.5% (4.3% / .2 = 21.5%), less the amount you paid in interest. The leverage created by a mortgage can make a huge difference in the return earned on your home. Mortgage interest may also provide an income tax deduction, depending upon your situation. A "free and clear" home is the equivalent of having a safe stuffed full of cash, but you can't find the combination to open it! In the next chapter, I'll provide that combination.

Figure 14-1 Median Sales Price of Homes 1980-2023

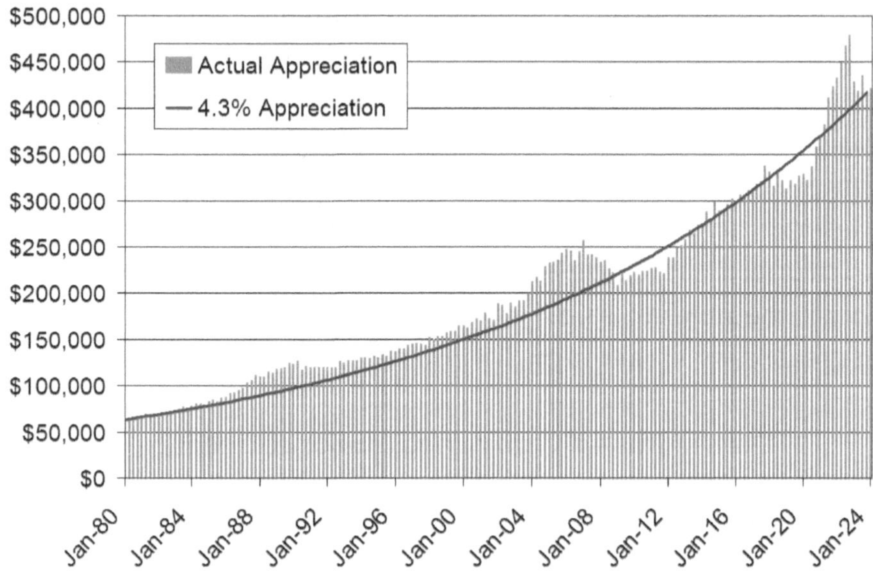

15

Reversing Your
Red Ink

"The most expensive thing you can own is a closed mind."
– Mimmo Fischetti

Inflation is especially hard on older Americans who retired 10 or 20 years ago on fixed incomes. The cost of food, fuel, utilities, insurance, taxes, maintenance, and repairs have all increased, but the cost-of-living increases from Social Security aren't enough to offset the increased costs.

Many retirees struggle to pay for basic needs, such as food and utilities. They often can't afford the gasoline to drive to see their children and grandchildren. What seemed like plenty when they retired is no longer enough to pay their bills. I've shown thousands of retirees how to use the equity in their home to offset inflation without losing their home to the bank.

A Home Equity Conversion Mortgage (HECM), commonly known as a *reverse mortgage*, enables seniors 62 or older to access some of their equity in their home. These loans are backed by the US Department of Housing and Urban Development (HUD). Reverse mortgages have nine unique features than aren't found in other loan programs:

No Payments – A reverse mortgage doesn't need to be repaid until the borrower sells the home, dies, or permanently moves away, but the property tax and insurance still need to be paid each year.

Easier Income Requirements – Because the loan is secured by *home equity*, you don't have to qualify for a monthly payment. However, there is a residual income requirement based upon the taxes, insurance, HOA dues, and any outstanding debts which must be paid each month. These obligations are subtracted from the borrower's current income and HUD requires a certain amount to be left over, which varies depending on where you live.

No Minimum Credit Score – Qualification for a HECM loan is *not* dependent on your credit score, but a two-year "look back" of your property tax, insurance, and HOA dues payment history is required. If you were late paying these items, a lender escrow set aside account may be required.

No Social Security or Medicare Impact – A reverse mortgage is a *loan*, and thus is not considered income that could impact your eligibility for Social Security or Medicare benefits.

No Income Tax Liability – A reverse mortgage is not a sale, so the equity received can be used by the homeowner for any purpose without incurring income tax.

No Maturity Date – HECM loans last as long as *you* do. If you get a reverse mortgage when you turn 62 and live to be 112, you will never have to move or make a payment on the loan as long as it remains your primary residence and property tax, insurance, HOA dues, and maintenance are kept current.

Non-Recourse – If you outlive the actuarial tables and owe more than your home is worth, the bank cannot hold you or your heirs liable for the deficit. You can continue to live in your home until you and your spouse both die. The bank can't call the loan due as long as you maintain the property and keep the taxes, insurance, and HOA dues paid.

Payment Plan Options – You can choose to receive a lump sum payout of your equity or the *tenure* option, which pays guaranteed monthly cash advances for as long as your home is the primary residence of at least one borrower. You also can choose to put the proceeds in a credit line which has a guaranteed growth rate. You have access to the funds whenever you need them. You can choose either a fixed interest rate or adjustable rate which changes over time.

Repayment – You can choose to make no payments and let the loan balance increase or make interest-only payments to keep the loan balance the same. You *could* opt to make amortized payments, but then a reverse mortgage is likely not the best option, as a traditional mortgage would be less costly to obtain.

Reverse mortgages are not new. The first reverse mortgage was issued in 1961 in Portland, Maine, by Nelson Hayes of Deering Savings & Loan. He created the loan to help Nellie Young, the widow of his high school football coach, stay in her home. It took decades before an FHA-insured version of this loan would become available, but the Reverse Mortgage Bill was signed into law in 1988 by President Ronald Reagan.

The biggest misconception people have about a reverse mortgage is that the bank will end up with their home instead of their children. For that to happen, you'd either have to live decades longer than the actuarial tables predict or the property value would have to decline substantially. If either of these things happened, you'd *win*, because you wouldn't be liable for the loss. The mortgage insurance company (not your heirs) would be responsible for absorbing the unlikely loss.

CHAPTER 15 – REVERSING YOUR RED INK

Unfortunately, there are misleading ads for reverse mortgages on television featuring former *Love Boat* actors stating, "Your house will pay you an allowance." Although the *term payment plan* will provide monthly payouts of your home's equity, you'd be essentially "eating" your home every month. What they don't tell you in the commercial is that the "allowance" often lasts only ten years. On the term payment plan, when you reach your equity limit, the payments stop! As you get older and your health declines, you'll likely need more money each month, not less! I encourage people to invest the equity from their home and eat the interest, rather than depleting the principal of their home.

A few years ago, I was contacted by clients I'd helped to purchase a home 22 years earlier. They were in their mid-70s and wanted me to help them sell their home. When I asked where they were moving, they were embarrassed to share that they had not been able to live on their retirement income and had run up more than $30,000 in credit card debt. They were struggling to make even the minimum payment each month.

Their intention was to sell their home, pay off their credit card debt, and rent a smaller home. I showed them that rent for a smaller home would be twice as much as their current mortgage payment. The equity from selling their home would be enough to pay off their credit card debt, but if they couldn't make ends meet with a $700 mortgage payment, selling their home and paying $1,600 in rent would make matters worse, increasing their monthly shortfall by $900. Within a year or two they would be in a worse predicament, with even higher credit card debt and no home equity.

Instead of selling their home to earn a commission, I contacted Tina Steele, a Tucson mortgage lender who specializes in reverse mortgages. I've known Tina for more than a decade. She is both knowledgeable and ethical, putting her client's needs before her own interests. Tina was able to help my clients get enough equity from their home to pay off their credit card debt *and* their existing mortgage.

Because a reverse mortgage requires no payments, the couple now has the $700 they previously paid on their mortgage and the $1,200 they were paying toward their credit card debt. The $1,900 difference each month ($22,800 per year) will enable them to enjoy a stress-free retirement living in their home with plenty of equity to leave to their children. A reverse mortgage is especially helpful in situations where one spouse passes away, leaving the surviving spouse to pay all the household bills with only one Social Security check. For this reason alone, if you haven't checked into a reverse mortgage, you should!

The government encourages reverse mortgages to help seniors access the equity in their home without adding a monthly expense. Your "dead" equity does nothing to help you or the economy, but if you *invest* it, generate interest income, and spend it, you create jobs for other taxpayers and a lifetime of memories for you and your family. As the popularity of HECM loans has grown, the limits have increased to keep up with home values. Figure 15-1 shows the limit history since 2009. The maximum loan amount is the lower of the HECM limit or the appraised value times the Loan To Value ratio (LTV) for your age in Figure 15-2.

Figure 15-1 HUD Lending Limits on HECM Loans

Year	HECM Limit	Increase	
		$	%
2009 - 2016	$625,500		
2017	$636,150	$10,650	1.7%
2018	$679,650	$43,500	6.8%
2019	$726,525	$46,875	6.9%
2020	$765,600	$39,075	5.4%
2021	$822,375	$56,775	7.4%
2022	$970,800	$148,425	18.0%
2023	$1,089,300	$118,500	12.2%
2024	$1,149,825	$60,525	5.6%

Reverse mortgages are expensive! In fact, they're one of the most expensive loans that banks offer. Unfortunately, the high commissions attract unscrupulous lenders looking for a quick commission. It's important to find a reputable lender who specializes in reverse mortgages and is willing to *walk away* from the commission if a HECM isn't right for you.

The mortgage insurance premium on a HECM loan is about 2% of the value of your home or maximum claim amount, whichever is less. For example, if the value of your home is $1,600,000, but the HECM limit is $1,149,825, the insurance premium is based on the lower amount. The fee is not 2% of the loan amount; it's 2% of the *value* of your home. If you own a $400,000 home and plan to get a reverse mortgage, the cost of the mortgage insurance would be $8,000. You'll also pay an annual premium of 0.5% of the amount outstanding. The cost of the loan compared to the amount of equity you can receive varies by age. The percentage of the appraised value you can receive is based upon your age. Figure 15-2 provides the equity you could withdraw for homes valued at $200,000, $400,000, $800,000 and the maximum of $1,149,825.

Figure 15-2 Reverse Mortgage Limits by Age in 2024

Age	LTV	HECM Loan Limit by Home Value & Age			
		$200,000	$400,000	$800,000	$1,149,825
62	35.0%	$70,000	$140,000	$280,000	$402,439
65	37.1%	$74,200	$148,400	$296,800	$426,585
70	40.8%	$81,600	$163,200	$326,400	$469,129
75	43.7%	$87,400	$174,800	$349,600	$502,474
80	48.1%	$96,200	$192,400	$384,800	$553,066
85	54.3%	$108,600	$217,200	$434,400	$624,355
90	61.3%	$122,600	$245,200	$490,400	$704,843

If you are not good at managing money, or plan to move in a few years, a reverse mortgage may not be a good option for you. However, if you're living in your *"forever"* home, it can be a lifesaver for many older Americans! In the next chapter, I'll share how to maximize the benefits of a reverse mortgage.

16

Double-Dipping Home Equity

"An investment in knowledge pays the best interest."
– Benjamin Franklin

When you receive a lump sum payment from your reverse mortgage, you don't want to spend it; you want to *invest* it and spend the interest. The perfect investment for your home equity is equity in someone else's home. At the beginning of 2024, 84 million homeowners in the United States had loans on their home. When a loan is originated, the borrowers sign a promissory note which documents their promise to repay the lender. This "note" is a legal document that outlines the terms to repay the loan, including the loan amount, interest rate, term, and payment schedule.

Promissory notes have been around since the Middle Ages, with the oldest recorded mortgage dating back to 1190 in England. The word 'mortgage' is a combination of two Latin words; 'mort' which means death and 'gage' which means pledge, so a mortgage is a *death pledge* that protects the creditor in the event the borrower dies before the loan is repaid.

Compound interest is the reason banks own the tallest buildings in most major cities of the world. Bank profits are made on the backs of retired people, but it doesn't have to be that way. If homeowners are going to pay interest to someone, why shouldn't they pay it to *you* instead of to the bank which is using your money to fund the borrower's loan?

Note investing is the fastest-growing type of real estate investing in the United States. In 2018, I published a book titled, *Who Needs the BANK?* to educate people about notes. In that book, I compared note investing to having your money in a bank, the stock market, and rental properties.

DOUBLE-DIPPING HOME EQUITY

When you're retired and no longer working, protecting your capital is of utmost importance. Notes often pay a much higher interest rate than banks do, and the collateral is a legally recorded lien secured by real estate. Investing locally allows you to drive by the property, establish the value, and even meet the borrowers if you like.

I don't know much about the companies selling their stock on Wall Street and would much rather fund the local "mom and pop" business owners on Main Street. Many business owners can't qualify for a bank loan, but *not* because they have bad credit or don't pay their bills on time. Most businesses have cycles which cause the business owners to earn their money in *spurts* instead of bi-weekly checks from an employer. Banks prefer to lend to those who *receive* paychecks, rather than to those who *sign* them.

Most of the people I lend to are self-employed business owners. They don't work 40 hours per week; it's more like 80 or 100 hours per week. They tend to have a strong work ethic, earn far more than an average borrower, and have a larger down payment than the W-2 employees approved by the bank.

Banks package their loans and sell them in bundles. Self-employed borrowers don't fall within the "one size fits all" mentality used by the bank, and are thus excluded because:

- Their income isn't consistent every month
- They work on tips or are paid in cash
- They take too many income tax deductions
- They have less than two years in their business

Notes provide a predictable monthly payment instead of the *hope* that your investment increases in the Wall Street casino. They are often set up on a 30-year payment schedule to make the payment affordable for the borrower. If you start at 62, the 360 monthly note payments would provide income for even the youngest reverse mortgage recipient every month until they are 92 years old (unless the note is paid off early).

With each monthly note payment, a small portion of the principal is repaid, reducing the amount you have invested. Although appreciation isn't linear, it still happens. As the value of the collateral (the borrower's home) *increases*, the balance of your note *decreases*, lowering your risk with each payment.

If the proceeds from a reverse mortgage are invested in notes, the monthly payments can be used to pay the tax, insurance, utilities, repairs, and maintenance on your home and vehicles. With these expenses covered, your Social Security income can be used as you intended - to enjoy a better lifestyle in retirement than you had while working.

Because a reverse mortgage requires no monthly payments, interest accrues each month, but appreciation also occurs. If you get a reverse mortgage when you are 62 years old, the loan limits in Figure 15-2 show the maximum loan amount in 2024 to be thirty-five percent of your home's value.

Interest would accrue on thirty-five percent of the home's value, but appreciation occurs on one hundred percent of the home's value. Figure 16-1 illustrates how the 62-year-old owners of a $400,000 home could benefit by investing the proceeds from a $140,000 (35% LTV) reverse mortgage into notes over thirty years. The calculation assumes the home appreciates at 4.3% per year, the interest rate on the reverse mortgage is 7% and the promissory note in which the proceeds are invested earns 7%.

Figure 16-1 Reverse Mortgage Over Time

REVERSE MORTGAGE EQUITY ESTIMATE					
Annual Home Appreciation 4.30%			Reverse Mortgage Interest Rate 7.00%		Note Investment — Interest 7.00% — Payment $931.42
Year	Age	Home Value	Loan Amount	Home Equity	Cum. Note Income	Note Balance
0	62	$400,000	$140,000	$260,000	$0	$140,000
1	63	$417,200	$150,121	$267,079	$11,177	$138,578
5	67	$493,721	$198,468	$295,253	$55,885	$131,784
10	72	$609,401	$281,353	$328,048	$111,771	$120,137
15	77	$752,185	$398,853	$353,332	$167,656	$103,626
20	82	$928,424	$565,423	$363,000	$223,542	$80,220
25	87	$1,145,955	$801,559	$344,397	$279,427	$47,039
30	92	$1,414,455	$1,136,310	$278,146	$335,312	$0

In this example, after five years, the retirees will have received 60 monthly payments of $931.42 for a total of $55,885.20. Because the majority of each payment is interest, the $140,000 promissory note is paid down by only $8,216 and the note still has $131,784 remaining. The retiree's equity in their home increases by $35,253 to $295,253.

After ten years, the retirees will have received 120 monthly payments of $931.42 for a total of $111,771. Most of the payment is still interest, so the $140,000 promissory note is paid down by only $19,863 and still has $120,137 remaining.

The retiree's equity in their home will have increased even more to $328,048.

After twenty years, the retirees will have received 240 monthly payments of $931.42 for a total of $223,542. The $140,000 promissory note is paid down by only $59,780 and still has $80,220 (more than half) remaining. The retiree's equity in their home is $363,000, which will start to decline in the last 10 years but is still $103,000 higher than the $260,000 equity when the reverse mortgage was initiated.

By the time the 30-year promissory note pays off, the homeowners will be 92 years old (if they funded the note at 62). The $140,000 note will have paid $335,311 over its term and the retirees will still have $278,146 in equity. The equity is $18,146 more than when they got the reverse mortgage. How much of a difference do you think the $335,312 made in their retirement lifestyle?

For many retired couples, it takes one spouse's Social Security check to pay the property taxes on their home and a good portion of the other spouse's check to pay the insurance, utilities, repairs, and maintenance. I've helped many seniors improve their lifestyle by investing their home equity in secure real estate notes. Using this strategy, clients who otherwise would have sold their homes to cover living expenses are now able to keep their home, pay off their debts, and earn monthly income which provides them with a much higher standard of living.

17

Noticing
Note Opportunities

*"Compound interest is the eighth wonder of the world.
He who understands it, earns it... he who doesn't... pays it."*
– Albert Einstein

Notes are all around you. According to the United States Census Bureau, 64.8% of American homeowners have a mortgage on their home. Through years of experience in dealing with a variety of housing problems, I found a niche in private lending in 2000. During the past twenty-five years, I have created, tested, and perfected my process and traveled the country to share this amazing opportunity with anyone who would listen.

The private lending process completes the circle for a *win-win-win* business model. Buyers get a home that the bank wouldn't allow them to buy, sellers get their home sold faster (and often without buyer concessions), and our retirees get secure investments with predictable monthly payments that enable them to enjoy a higher standard of living. The win-win-win benefits of private lending are outlined below for the borrower, home seller, and retirees who fund the notes.

<u>BORROWER BENEFITS</u>

Buyers get a loan that traditional lenders won't allow them to have. Instead of paying off their landlord's mortgage in a rental, they can create their own wealth through the American dream of home ownership. The monthly payment to *own* a home is often less than the cost of rent, creating an immediate cash surplus for the borrower each month.

In addition to a lower monthly payment, homeowners may be able to deduct mortgage interest and property tax to reduce their income tax liability. The additional tax deductions can increase the amount of their paycheck, adding even more to their monthly cash surplus. However, as mentioned in

Chapter 14, the biggest benefit for the buyer is the leverage provided by the loan. If the home appreciates in value, the borrowers receive it all, even though their down payment was only a fraction of the home's value.

HOME SELLER BENEFITS

When sellers offer financing on their home, they'll usually get a higher price, a faster sale, and pay no concessions for the buyers. In addition to these benefits, they can earn a much higher interest rate than banks or other investments pay. There are also income tax benefits to taking the profit from the sale *over time*, instead of receiving a lump sum payment. The security and flexibility of notes make them easy to sell.

Landlords who sell their properties and finance their buyers often receive more each month from owning the *paper* than they ever received while owning the *property*. They avoid the "tenant and toilet" hassles of being a landlord, repairman, janitor, and marriage counselor, while no longer being responsible for taxes, insurance, repairs, maintenance, and vacancy.

RETIREE BENEFITS

Many sellers are unable to offer financing on their home because they need the money to pay off their loan and buy their next home. This is where retirees can step in and buy the note from the seller at the closing table. Many retirees don't think of themselves as real estate investors, but when they finance notes secured by real estate, that's exactly what they become.

Most of the retirees who've funded real estate notes for our clients had their cash sitting in a bank earning little or no interest. Their money was being devalued by inflation. Notes secured by the borrower's home offer payments that are more than enough to offset the devastating effects of inflation. They provide a steady stream of predictable monthly income without the volatility of the stock market or the headaches of being a landlord.

Banks are in the business of providing loans, but most sell them as soon as they fund them to free up the capital for more loans. The completed loans are bundled into packages and sold to Fannie Mae, Freddie Mac, large banks, insurance companies, or hedge funds, which are collectively referred to as the secondary market.

These loan-buying entities require certain criteria of the loans they buy. Every month, banks turn down thousands of qualified borrowers who don't have the consistent income required by the secondary market. Many jump to the conclusion that if a person can't get a bank loan, they must have bad credit or be a bad risk. Borrowers who have the discipline to save 15% to 50% for a down payment make really good candidates for private loans.

There are dozens of internet websites that sell real estate notes but be very careful about buying notes from strangers. There's a lot of overpriced "junk" paper for sale by unscrupulous people who cut corners. Many of the notes I've seen for sale were not drafted by an attorney, not closed at a title company, and the borrowers were not qualified by a licensed lender. Often times, the borrower's down payment was low or non-existent and the collateral isn't worth as much as they're asking for the note. There are also scammers who try to buy notes for far less or sell them for far more than a reputable investor would pay.

If possible, try to lend locally and partner with someone who has a good reputation in your town. You can establish a working relationship with them and create years of trouble-free payments. Before you fund any borrowers, be sure to ask for referrals from other lenders with whom they've had loans. It isn't easy to find someone who values your money as much as you do, but they're out there. Integrity is one of the most important qualities to look for in a borrower.

If you're going to fund notes in a market outside of your locality, it's very important to have someone you know and trust who lives near the property. They can view the property, meet the people, and let you know if the price is competitive for the area. Bad things happen to good people, so it's important to have someone with "boots on the ground" where the property is located so they can jump in to help if needed.

There are several other things that can be done to limit your risk. Be sure that the notes you fund were drafted by an attorney in the state where the property is located. If the borrowers are owner-occupants, they need to be qualified by a licensed loan originator to ensure that they have the ability to repay the loan. The borrower should also use their own money to make a down payment of at least 15%. The transaction should always be closed at a title company with the note insured by title insurance. The loan should be professionally serviced to ensure that the property tax and hazard insurance are paid. It's also good to have the payment history from a third party, not just the note seller, who assures you that, "The borrower always pays on time."

If you're new to note investing, I suggest going to local investor club meetings. It's good to partner with someone who lives locally, is experienced, has a good reputation, and has already participated in several real estate notes. Partnering with someone else may not produce as high of a return, but it will familiarize you with the process, while limiting your exposure and keeping you from buying someone else's bad notes. If someone gave you this book, contact them to find out if they have any local note investing opportunities available. If you can't find anyone locally, email *bob@notecarry.com*. I have a vast network of friends and may know of someone experienced and trustworthy in your area.

I use retirees in examples throughout this book because they've had more time to save than the younger generations. You don't have to be retired to own notes. In fact, I have a good friend whose grandchild inherited a Roth IRA at six months old and has owned notes ever since!

Notes are great investments for self-directed Coverdell Educational Savings Accounts, Health Savings Accounts, Roth IRAs, and Roth 401(k)s, all of which provide tax-free returns. You can also purchase notes in self-directed 401(k) and Individual Retirement Accounts, or with money you have in the bank, stock market, home equity, or under your mattress.

18

Slow and Steady Wins the Race

*"Patience is not simply the ability to wait;
it's how we behave while we're waiting."*
— *Joyce Meyer*

As you age, you have less and less time to recover from losses in the stock market. With each monthly note payment you receive, a small portion of the principal is repaid, lowering the amount you have invested in the note. As the value of the property increases, your note investment becomes more *secure*. A benefit of funding notes on affordable homes is that these properties typically appreciate faster than others due to the low supply and the high demand for affordable housing. Figure 18-1 illustrates the declining risk in the first 10 years of a 30-year note for $140,000 on a $200,000 property.

Figure 18-1 Declining Loan To Value (LTV) Over Time

| Year | PROPERTY | | NOTE | | Loan to Value Ratio (LTV) |
	4.00% Property Apprec.	Year End Value of Property	7.00% Principal Paid	Year End Balance of Note	
0	-	$200,000	-	$140,000	70.0%
1	$8,000	$208,000	$1,422	$138,578	66.6%
2	$8,320	$216,320	$1,430	$137,147	63.4%
3	$8,653	$224,973	$1,439	$135,709	60.3%
4	$8,999	$233,972	$1,447	$134,261	57.4%
5	$9,359	$243,331	$1,456	$132,806	54.6%
6	$9,733	$253,064	$1,464	$131,342	51.9%
7	$10,123	$263,186	$1,473	$129,869	49.3%
8	$10,527	$273,714	$1,481	$128,388	46.9%
9	$10,949	$284,662	$1,490	$126,898	44.6%
10	$11,386	$296,049	$1,499	$125,399	42.4%

The $140,000 note is 70% of the home value, so the loan to value ratio (LTV) is 70%. By the third year of the loan, the LTV ratio is 60.3%, and in the 7th year it drops below half to 49.3%.

SLOW AND STEADY WINS THE RACE

For someone on a fixed income, funding only 70% of a home's value provides a 30% cushion in the event of a market downturn. The property pledged as collateral could lose 30% of its value, before *any* of your capital is at risk. What other investments could lose nearly one-third of their value, without you losing any of your money?

You can find notes that pay more than 7% interest, but they'll likely have a higher LTV, and thus, more risk. Your tolerance for risk will help you determine which notes are best for you, but if you're no longer working, you may not have the ability to replenish lost capital. I like a high return as much as anyone, but it's not wise to take risks with your retirement savings. When what you have saved is all you'll *ever have*, it's crucial that you protect it.

If you had the choice between funding a long-term note paying 7% and a short-term note for a fix & flip investor offering 12%, most people would opt to fund the 12% note with the house flipper. An important thing to remember about lending is that risk and reward go hand-in-hand; the higher the rate, the higher the *risk*. There's always a reason when borrowers offer to pay a high interest rate.

The reasons the rate is higher on fix & flips loans are because: 1) the loan will be paid off in a short period of time, and 2) the loan is risky. The day you fund the loan, the borrower intentionally begins to destroy the home so they can rebuild it with modern amenities. What if they die or don't finish the job? The four notes I've had to foreclose on were all house flippers who didn't finish what they started.

A note of $100,000 at 12% would pay $12,000 in interest per year, which is $1,000 per month. If the home is renovated and sold after three months, you'd receive a total of $3,000 for risking $100,000. After the loan is paid off, the money sits in your bank account until you find another project to fund. If it takes three months to fund another note, you'd earn another $3,000 for the second three-month note.

At the end of the year, you will have earned $6,000 in interest, which is only 6% of the $100,000 you risked *twice!* Funding a 7% long-term note for a landlord or homeowner not only pays more; it's less risky. Your money is working every day of the year instead of sitting idle half the time. You also avoid the risk of ending up with a gutted-out house if the fix & flip contractor gets hit by a bus.

Earlier in my career, when things didn't go as expected, our long-time assistant and friend, Marianne Kartsonis, would jokingly say, "Man plans, and God laughs!" Even the most experienced fix & flip investors run into unexpected issues like cost overruns, permit delays, contractors not showing up, etc. These delays can be the difference between making a profit or suffering a loss. If your LTV ratio is too high, their loss could become *yours!*

If I was younger, I'd start a new contracting business and call it *The Last Ten Percent*. The company would complete the work contractors didn't finish. I'm not sure why, but many people in the trades seem to stop showing up when the final touch up work needs to be done. Is it because it's not as exciting as erecting new walls or because they underbid the job? I'm not sure why, but after the original contractors have moved on, the owners are *bleeding* money on an unfinished home, so someone could earn a lot to finish the job.

Markets can change dramatically due to interest rate fluctuations, natural disasters, military base closures, layoffs, or expansions. In a matter of months, the housing market can shift from bidding wars to homes not even being shown. Few fix & flip contractors budget for six months or a year of carrying costs. Many who haven't been in business very long would not recognize the signs of a down market because there wasn't a downturn between 2012 and 2024.

The carrying costs (mortgage, tax, insurance, utilities, etc.) on an empty home are about 2% of the home's value each month. If a home doesn't sell in 5 months, the house flipper's 10% profit that wasn't eaten by delays and overages will be consumed in carrying costs. When the house flipper has lost all of their profit, they can't lower the price without bringing money to the closing table. Depending on their financial condition, their problem could easily become *your* problem.

I often tease flippers that they're not investors at all! Flipping is a *job* and it's the worst job in the world! You have to pay money to get the job, it costs money every day you have the job, and when you finally get your first paycheck, the job ends and you're *fired!* With each new flip you fund, you have to conduct due diligence on the property *and* the borrower. I like to fund long-term loans because I don't want to put my investment capital at risk every few months.

Many retirees like the idea of short-term notes and balk at the idea of funding 30-year notes. They tell me, "I'll be dead before the note pays off." I ask them to name the people they know who've lived in their home for 30 years. People usually sell their home well before the loan matures and the note can be sold if you need the money. If you had a $100,000 note at 7% for 30 years, it would pay $665.30 per month. How many of your friends would like to receive that check every month?

In my experience, most families have at least one child who isn't good at managing money. Notes held in a trust can provide a monthly allowance for decades to keep your heirs from blowing their inheritance within a few months of your funeral. Notes can provide parents with peace of mind, knowing that their financially challenged children will be ok after they're gone.

Notes have been a godsend for many of my real estate clients. I don't earn a commission on the notes I help to fund because I'm not a licensed securities dealer. But by doing what's best for my clients, I've gotten a lot of referrals and new lenders for our hard-working, self-employed clients who can't get bank loans to purchase a home.

My "set it and forget it" philosophy is to conduct due diligence *once* and get paid for decades. It defies logic that lower interest notes can actually pay more than high interest notes, but consistency is underrated. The tortoise and hare in Aesop's Fables taught us that slow and steady wins the race!

19

Reducing Your Risk

"Ben Franklin may have discovered electricity- but it is the man who invented the meter who made the money."
— *Earl Warren*

There's a saying in the note business, "Don't make the *loan* if you don't want to *own!*" People die, get divorced, or can disappear, so it's important to think about what you'd do if something like that happened. Simply *knowing* someone doesn't relieve you of the responsibility to perform due diligence. It's your job to ensure that protections are taken with each investment to preserve your capital.

A good question to ask before funding a note is, "What percentage of the American population would buy this property if I had to sell it?" If you are funding a large apartment complex or commercial building, the answer might be a very low, single-digit percentage, which is not good. The value of real estate is a function of supply and demand. Rural properties, homes on busy streets, and those with strange floor plans have smaller buyer pools. Properties with low demand often take longer to sell and require a discounted price.

I invest in affordable single-family homes because there's a shortage of affordable housing. If I ended up with the home, I could easily sell it to first-time home buyers, downsizing retirees, vacation rental hosts, long-term landlords, or Wall Street hedge funds that buy affordable homes. That gives me five exit strategies in the event I'd need them.

Investors sometimes ask to make interest-only payments instead of amortized payments, which include both principal and interest. The benefit to them is a lower payment, but it also lowers *your* payment. Interest-only payments add risk because in declining markets, the loan amount remains the same as the home value declines, increasing the LTV and your risk.

After more than four decades of investing in real estate, I know that prices don't always increase. In 2013, the Federal Housing Finance Agency released the results from a study of the foreclosures that occurred during the 2008 financial crisis from 2007 - 2013. The study found that a borrower's credit score wasn't the best determinant of whether they'd pay their mortgage. In fact, there were foreclosures across all Fair Isaac Corporation (FICO) credit scores, even those above 800.

The study found that the down payment was directly correlated to the likelihood that a loan would fail. Those whose down payment was 15% of the purchase price or more had less than a 1% fallout rate per year during the worst seven years since the Great Depression. For this reason, I want borrowers to pay at least 15% down and make fully-amortized payments on the notes I fund. When the borrowers have more to lose every month than I do, I'll have a lot lower chance of failure.

Investors often try to maximize their return by investing as little as possible. When their profit is calculated on a smaller investment, the yield will be higher, but the less the borrower puts down, the higher the risk is to the lender. I've found that it is better to fund notes with a higher down payment and a lower interest rate. Making the payment more affordable for the homeowner results in a more reliable income stream.

There are more lending opportunities in lower-priced markets than in higher-priced markets. When homes are affordable for more people, demand is higher. You can often earn a higher interest rate and still provide borrowers with a payment that's lower than rent.

Most people will experience an unanticipated expense at some time in their life such as a car accident, illness, layoff, or other financial setback. When borrowers are short on money, they look for someone they don't have to pay. I want them to look out the window and realize that the home across the street costs more money to *rent* than the amount they pay me to *own* the one they're in. An affordable payment for the borrower ensures that I'll be paid. The consequence of not paying me is moving and paying someone else more.

The two things that can adversely affect your first position note (first in priority to be paid) are if the taxes aren't paid or if the property is destroyed by fire or another disaster when it isn't insured. Property tax is the only lien that can take priority on a first position note. This is why we hire a note servicing company to collect the taxes and insurance each month and pay them when they are due.

There's usually nothing on a note that allows you to determine whether it is in 1st position or 2nd position. The position of a note is the order in which it's recorded at the County Recorder's office. The time stamp placed on the document by the County Recorder determines what position the note is in to be paid. A lien in 1st position receives all of its interest and principal before a lien in 2nd position gets a penny. It's important to know your position and have the borrower buy title insurance to protect it.

With note investing, you do the work once and are paid for decades until the note pays off. Don't deviate from your lending guidelines. In my book, *"Who Needs the BANK?"* I provided a checklist of the items you should have before funding notes, and I included the due diligence that should be done before investing. The character of the person borrowing the money is just as important to me as the market value of the property.

The promissory note that spells out the terms of the loan is a private document between the borrower and the lender that is not recorded in public view. Depending on where you live, either a deed of trust or a mortgage secures your position to be paid. The document is recorded by the County Recorder of the county in which the property is situated.

State laws in about half of the United States require a mortgage to secure the loan and the other half allow a deed of trust. Nine states allow either document and allow the lender to choose which is used. It's important to know the difference between these documents because they determine what happens if the buyer doesn't repay as promised.

Mortgages are two-party agreements between the lender and the borrower. In the event of a dispute, the matter is resolved by a judge. A deed of trust is a three-party agreement which establishes a trustee to act as referee of the transaction. The trustee is often a local attorney or title company whose job is to follow the terms of the note. The deed is held by the trustee. If the borrower repays the loan, the trustee gives the deed to the borrower and records a lien release. If the borrower dies, or for some reason doesn't pay the loan as agreed, the lender can foreclose on the property. If this happens, the trustee gives the deed to the note holder.

Where you lend matters! Each state has an established foreclosure timeline if a borrower defaults on their payments. In the states that require a judicial foreclosure, the process tends to take a lot longer because it must go through the court system and can be subject to delays due to hearings, judge's schedules, backlogs, and extensions. Before you fund a note, be sure to find out how long it takes to foreclose in the state where the property is located.

The benefits of owning notes are many, but one of the best is the lack of *liability*. There are two kinds of people in this world: "makers" and "takers." Unfortunately, there seem to be a lot more frivolous lawsuits, squatters, and people looking to take things from you each year. If an unfortunate accident happens on a rental property you *own*, you're likely to be sued. If you are the lender on the property, your lien was already recorded in first position before the accident happened and the lawsuit was filed. Even if the landlord loses the lawsuit and a judgment is placed on the property, you will still be the first to be paid when the property is sold.

The four properties we've foreclosed on all were all fix & flip contractors. We ended up selling each home for more than we would have gotten if the borrowers repaid the note as promised. How many investments can you think of where the worst case scenario pays *more* than the best case scenario? Offering home loans to those who can't obtain bank mortgages but have good income, credit, and down payment, has unlocked new income streams for many of our friends, family, real estate clients, and NoteCarry coaching members.

20

Avoiding Stock Shock

The Baby Boom generation is defined as people born between 1946 and 1964. About 80 million Boomers were born in the United States, and in 2011 they began turning 65 years old. Approximately 10,000 Americans turn 65 years old *every single day!* That's 300,000 people per month and 3.6 million people each year! When the last of the Baby Boomers turn 65 in 2029, even more people will reach retirement age every day because the Millennial generation is even larger!

When people reach retirement age and stop working, the stock market is affected in two ways: 1) Retirees stop putting money *in,* and 2) They begin taking money *out.* In a free market economy, the value of any commodity is a function of supply and demand. As thousands of people every day stop *buying* stocks, and instead start *selling* them to cover monthly living expenses, demand declines. The Millennial children of the Baby Boomers aren't saving nearly as much as their parents did. Many of these financially-challenged children are referred to as *waiters;* not because they have jobs in restaurants, but because their only financial plan is *waiting* for their parents to die! When that happens, they'll sell the stocks even faster.

With fewer buyers and more sellers, the supply of stocks will likely increase as demand for the shares decreases. I don't want to roll the dice in the Wall Street casino with my ability to retire on the line. When you're young and retirement is decades away, you may be able to stomach the volatility of the stock market, but that changes once you have retired. You no longer have the luxury of waiting for the market to recover when you need to sell shares every month to pay your living expenses.

Dollar cost averaging is when you invest the same amount each month and are able to buy more shares when the stock price is low and fewer shares when the price is high. When you retire and need a fixed amount to pay your bills each month, you will be forced to sell *more* shares when the stock price is low and *less* shares when the price is high. This is the opposite of dollar cost averaging.

Retirees who gamble with their life savings often panic when stock prices fall, selling at a loss. The price will likely come back, but they can't afford to take the risk and never should have risked their money in the first place. Their attempt to increase their nest egg backfires and they often end up with less than they initially invested.

The Standard and Poor's 500 (S&P 500) stock index tracks the share prices of 500 of the largest companies in the United States. Figure 20-1 shows how a retiree who invested $100,000 in the S&P 500 from 2000 to 2023 would have fared, assuming that they withdrew 4% of their account value at the end of each year. The total return for each year was obtained from: *https://www.slickcharts.com/sp500/returns*.

On the opposing page, Figure 20-2 shows how much the same $100,000 would produce during the same period of time if invested in real estate notes paying 7%. Both scenarios assume that the profits were reinvested at the end of the year after deducting 4% of the account balance for living expenses. Both investments grew during the 24-year period, both paid out more than was invested, and both had an ending balance higher than the $100,000 initially invested.

Figure 20-1 – $100,000 Invested in S&P 500 2000-2023

S&P 500					
Starting Investment in January, 2000					$100,000
Year	Start	Yield	Gain/Loss	4.00%	End
2000	$100,000	-9.10%	($9,100)	($3,636)	$87,264
2001	$87,264	-11.89%	($10,376)	($3,076)	$73,813
2002	$73,813	-22.10%	($16,313)	($2,300)	$55,200
2003	$55,200	28.68%	$15,831	($2,841)	$68,190
2004	$68,190	10.88%	$7,419	($3,024)	$72,585
2005	$72,585	4.91%	$3,564	($3,046)	$73,103
2006	$73,103	15.79%	$11,543	($3,386)	$81,260
2007	$81,260	5.49%	$4,461	($3,429)	$82,292
2008	$82,292	-37.00%	($30,448)	($2,074)	$49,770
2009	$49,770	26.46%	$13,169	($2,518)	$60,422
2010	$60,422	15.06%	$9,100	($2,781)	$66,741
2011	$66,741	2.11%	$1,408	($2,726)	$65,423
2012	$65,423	16.00%	$10,468	($3,036)	$72,855
2013	$72,855	32.39%	$23,598	($3,858)	$92,595
2014	$92,595	13.69%	$12,676	($4,211)	$101,060
2015	$101,060	1.38%	$1,395	($4,098)	$98,357
2016	$98,357	11.96%	$11,763	($4,405)	$105,715
2017	$105,715	21.83%	$23,078	($5,152)	$123,641
2018	$123,641	-4.38%	($5,415)	($4,729)	$113,497
2019	$113,497	31.49%	$35,740	($5,969)	$143,267
2020	$143,267	18.40%	$26,361	($6,785)	$162,843
2021	$162,843	28.71%	$46,752	($8,384)	$201,212
2022	$201,212	-18.11%	($36,439)	($6,591)	$158,182
2023	$158,182	26.29%	$41,586	($7,991)	$191,777
Total Paid / Total Earned				($100,044)	$291,821

An investment in the S&P 500 would have paid out $100,044 to the retirees and have $191,777 left over for a total of $291,821.

Figure 20-2 – $100,000 Invested in 7% Notes 2000-2023

7% Note					
Starting Investment in January, 2000					$100,000
Year	Start	Yield	Gain/Loss	4.00%	End
2000	$100,000	7.00%	$7,000	($4,280)	$102,720
2001	$102,720	7.00%	$7,190	($4,396)	$105,514
2002	$105,514	7.00%	$7,386	($4,516)	$108,384
2003	$108,384	7.00%	$7,587	($4,639)	$111,332
2004	$111,332	7.00%	$7,793	($4,765)	$114,360
2005	$114,360	7.00%	$8,005	($4,895)	$117,471
2006	$117,471	7.00%	$8,223	($5,028)	$120,666
2007	$120,666	7.00%	$8,447	($5,165)	$123,948
2008	$123,948	7.00%	$8,676	($5,305)	$127,320
2009	$127,320	7.00%	$8,912	($5,449)	$130,783
2010	$130,783	7.00%	$9,155	($5,597)	$134,340
2011	$134,340	7.00%	$9,404	($5,750)	$137,994
2012	$137,994	7.00%	$9,660	($5,906)	$141,747
2013	$141,747	7.00%	$9,922	($6,067)	$145,603
2014	$145,603	7.00%	$10,192	($6,232)	$149,563
2015	$149,563	7.00%	$10,469	($6,401)	$153,631
2016	$153,631	7.00%	$10,754	($6,575)	$157,810
2017	$157,810	7.00%	$11,047	($6,754)	$162,103
2018	$162,103	7.00%	$11,347	($6,938)	$166,512
2019	$166,512	7.00%	$11,656	($7,127)	$171,041
2020	$171,041	7.00%	$11,973	($7,321)	$175,693
2021	$175,693	7.00%	$12,299	($7,520)	$180,472
2022	$180,472	7.00%	$12,633	($7,724)	$185,381
2023	$185,381	7.00%	$12,977	($7,934)	$190,423
Total Paid / Total Earned				**($142,284)**	**$332,707**

An investment in a 7% Note would have paid out $142,284 to the retirees and have $190,423 left over for a total of $332,707.

The graph in Figure 20-3 shows that both investments start and end nearly the same after 24 years. The S&P 500 investment took 16 years to recover from losses in 2000-2002. During that time, the retirees with the 7% note would have received $42,240 more in withdrawals. The value of the S&P 500 at the end of 2023 was $1,354 higher than the note account.

Figure 20-3 S&P 500 vs. 7% Notes from 2000 to 2023

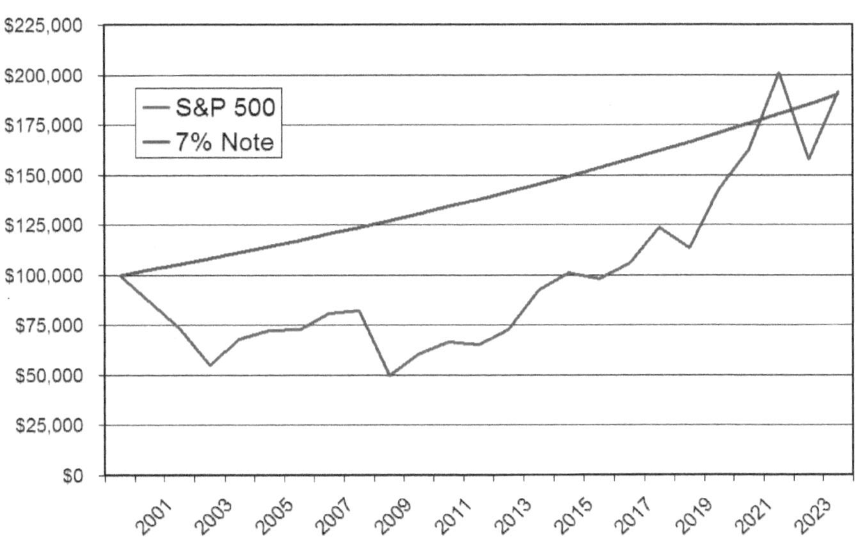

This analysis will vary widely if the dates are adjusted, but that's the point of this exercise. Are you willing to have your retirement lifestyle being dependent on the *day* you choose to invest or withdraw your money? How many sleepless nights did the retirees who invested in the S&P 500 experience during this time? The note holders received the same amount every month for 24 years and had nothing to worry about. If the borrowers stopped paying, the note holder would foreclose and end up with a home worth far more than they invested. I chose this path for my retirement savings.

21

Increasing Your Retirement Income

"How many millionaires do you know who have become wealthy by investing in savings accounts?"
— Robert G. Allen

Using ratios to determine how much an average family allocates toward their home, cars, IRA, 401(k), stocks, bonds, bank accounts, life insurance, etc. each month is *difficult!* We all spend money differently. Some own modest homes and drive their cars for decades while others upgrade their home and vehicles every few years. Some eat out and buy expensive clothing while others eat at home and shop at discount stores. Some are married with two incomes while others are single or only have one income. Some have children while others don't, and some save a lot while others don't save at all.

Averages can be misleading because one abnormally high or low data point can significantly skew the result. For example, if nine people on your street own homes valued at $100,000 and a home worth $10,000,000 is constructed, the average value for the neighborhood would be $1,090,000. In this example, the average is over *ten times higher* than nine of the ten homes on the street. The median price is a much better indicator than the average price when determining what is *normal* for the neighborhood.

The United States Census Bureau regularly publishes a report titled, *The Wealth of Households.* The June 2023, report showed the *median* household wealth (assets minus liabilities) in the United States at the end of 2021 was $166,900. Half the households had less and half had more. The lowest 25% had a net worth of $16,560 or less and the lowest 10% had either $0 or a negative net worth (more liabilities than assets). The top 10% of households had an average of $1,623,000 -almost ten times the median. Wealth distribution is much like the home values discussed earlier. The average doesn't tell the real story.

Instead of using either the average or median, I've opted to use *tables* throughout this chapter to make it easier to determine how much note income could be created based on the value of *your* assets. Figure 21-1 shows how much equity a Home Equity Conversion Mortgage (HECM) could provide based on your age and home value. The shaded row under each loan amount shows the monthly payment you will receive if the proceeds are invested in 30-year notes at 7% interest.

Figure 21-1 HECM Amount & Potential Note Income

Age	LTV / Note	Appraised Value of Home				
		$200,000	$400,000	$600,000	$800,000	$1,000,000
65	37.10%	$74,200	$148,400	$222,600	$296,800	$371,000
	7.00%	$494	$987	$1,481	$1,975	$2,468
70	40.80%	$81,600	$163,200	$244,800	$326,400	$408,000
	7.00%	$543	$1,086	$1,629	$2,172	$2,714
75	43.70%	$87,400	$174,800	$262,200	$349,600	$437,000
	7.00%	$581	$1,163	$1,744	$2,326	$2,907
80	48.10%	$96,200	$192,400	$288,600	$384,800	$481,000
	7.00%	$640	$1,280	$1,920	$2,560	$3,200
85	54.30%	$108,600	$217,200	$325,800	$434,400	$543,000
	7%	$723	$1,445	$2,168	$2,890	$3,613
90	61.30%	$122,600	$245,200	$367,800	$490,400	$613,000
	7.00%	$816	$1,631	$2,447	$3,263	$4,078

A 65-year-old who owns a $200,000 home could get a loan of $74,200, invest the proceeds in a note at 7%, and receive $494 per month for 30 years. A 90-year-old with a $1,000,000 home could get a loan of $613,000, invest it in *several* notes at 7% and receive payments of $4,078 per month for 30 years. You probably won't live to be 120, so when you die, your heirs can sell your home and either continue to receive the monthly note payments or sell them to other retirees who need extra income.

Chapter 6 discussed withdrawing extra money from your IRA to pay income tax each year. Chapter 7 discussed Required Minimum Distributions (RMDs) which could affect Social Security and Medicare payments. Chapter 8 covered the advantage of rolling over Traditional IRAs into Roth IRAs. In this chapter, I'll share why it may be better to "bite the bullet" and roll over your tax-deferred Traditional IRA funds into a Roth IRA upfront to avoid RMDs in the future.

Figure 21-2 assumes you have $100,000 earning 7% in a retirement account that hasn't been taxed. The interest in the first year would be $7,000, bringing your total to $107,000. Assuming you withdraw 4% of the total ($4,280) to live on in the first year and increase it by 4% for inflation every year after, your money will last 30 years. If you start in your 66th year, your income will last until you are 95 years old.

Figure 21-2 Value of Traditional IRA Over 35 Years

Year	Age	Starting Value	7% Interest	4% Withdrawn	22% Income Tax	Ending Value
1	66	$100,000	$7,000	-$4,280	-$942	$101,778
2	67	$101,778	$7,124	-$4,451	-$979	$103,472
3	68	$103,472	$7,243	-$4,629	-$1,018	$105,068
4	69	$105,068	$7,355	-$4,814	-$1,059	$106,549
5	70	$106,549	$7,458	-$5,007	-$1,102	$107,899
10	75	$111,588	$7,811	-$6,092	-$1,340	$111,967
15	80	$110,455	$7,732	-$7,412	-$1,631	$109,145
20	85	$98,888	$6,922	-$9,017	-$1,984	$94,809
25	90	$70,526	$4,937	-$10,971	-$2,414	$62,078
30	95	$15,977	$1,118	-$13,348	-$2,937	$811
35	100	$0	$0	$0	$0	$0
Total Over 30 Years =		$239,175		$239,175 Withdrawn	-$52,810 Income Tax	$0 Left Over

Your withdrawals will increase each year from $4,280 in the 1st year to $13,348 in the 30th year. The $100,000 will provide income of $239,175 before it runs out, but your income tax liability also increases each year. At a 22% tax rate, you would pay $52,810 in income tax before your account is depleted.

Figure 21-3 assumes the same $100,000 is rolled over into a Roth IRA and you pay the 22% income tax ($22,000) upfront from the account. It would be far better *not* to use your tax-free funds to pay the $22,000 income tax, but in this example, we assume you don't have other funds to pay the tax. If you earn 7% on the $78,000 remaining in your account and follow the same withdrawal schedule (4% the first year with a 4% increase every year), your money will *never run out!* You receive $245,881 which is $6,706 *more*, pay $30,810 *less* tax, and still have $83,804 left over when you reach the age of 100.

Figure 21-3 Value of Roth IRA With Tax Deducted

Year	Age	Starting Value	7% Interest	4% Withdrawn	0% Income Tax	Ending Value
1	66	$78,000	$5,460	-$3,338	$0	$80,122
2	67	$80,122	$5,609	-$3,472	$0	$82,258
3	68	$82,258	$5,758	-$3,611	$0	$84,405
4	69	$84,405	$5,908	-$3,755	$0	$86,559
5	70	$86,559	$6,059	-$3,905	$0	$88,712
10	75	$97,202	$6,804	-$4,752	$0	$99,255
15	80	$106,887	$7,482	-$5,781	$0	$108,588
20	85	$114,092	$7,986	-$7,034	$0	$115,045
25	90	$116,436	$8,151	-$8,557	$0	$116,029
30	95	$110,281	$7,720	-$10,411	$0	$107,589
35	100	$90,160	$6,311	-$12,667	$0	$83,804
TOTAL BENEFIT		$329,685	$245,881 Withdrawn	$0 Income Tax	$83,804 Left Over	

It takes 15 years to recover the income tax paid upfront, but after that, the untaxed Roth IRA account easily outpaces the taxable Traditional IRA account. What if you paid the income tax with other funds to keep the entire amount of your IRA earning tax-free interest in your Roth IRA?

It would make sense to use a reverse mortgage or other non-IRA funds to pay the income tax owed instead of using the funds in the tax-advantaged account. Income from notes purchased with your reverse mortgage proceeds is taxable, but notes purchased inside your Roth IRA are not. Figure 21-4 assumes the same withdrawal schedule as the two previous examples but starts the value of the Roth IRA at $100,000 instead of $78,000.

Figure 21-4 Value of Roth IRA Without Tax Deducted

Year	Age	Starting Value	7% Interest	4% Withdrawn	0% Income Tax	Ending Value
1	66	$100,000	$7,000	-$4,280	$0	$102,720
2	67	$102,720	$7,190	-$4,451	$0	$105,459
3	68	$105,459	$7,382	-$4,629	$0	$108,212
4	69	$108,212	$7,575	-$4,814	$0	$110,973
5	70	$110,973	$7,768	-$5,007	$0	$113,734
10	75	$124,618	$8,723	-$6,092	$0	$127,250
15	80	$137,035	$9,592	-$7,412	$0	$139,216
20	85	$146,272	$10,239	-$9,017	$0	$147,494
25	90	$149,277	$10,449	-$10,971	$0	$148,756
30	95	$141,386	$9,897	-$13,348	$0	$137,935
35	100	$115,590	$8,091	-$16,240	$0	$107,441
Total Over 30 Years =			$422,673	$315,232 Withdrawn	$0 Income Tax	$107,441 Left Over

With the full amount rolled into your Roth IRA, you will receive $315,323, which is $76,057 *more* than the Traditional

IRA pays, owe $30,810 *less* tax, and still have $107,441 left over when you reach 100, instead of running out of money at age 95.

Whether this is a good option for you depends on how long you live. If you can pay the income tax without depleting the funds in the IRA account, you should probably roll it over before they take that option away. However, if you don't think you have long to live, it may be better to pay the tax each year and transfer a higher amount to your heirs when you die. However, don't forget that RMDs force you to withdraw a higher amount each year and that could impact the amount you receive from Social Security and Medicare. Consult a financial professional to determine your best course of action.

Chapter 13 discussed how investing the money saved by not buying new vehicles could create interest income every month. Figure 21-5 provides the monthly principal and interest payments you will receive for 30 years if the money is invested at 7% instead of being spent on vehicles.

Figure 21-5 Note Income From Not Upgrading Vehicles

Amount Invested	$10,000	$20,000	$30,000	$40,000	$50,000
Interest rate	7.00%	7.00%	7.00%	7.00%	7.00%
Term (months)	360	360	360	360	360
Income / month	$66.53	$133.06	$199.59	$266.12	$332.65
Income / year	$798	$1,597	$2,395	$3,193	$3,992
Income - 10 yrs.	$7,984	$15,967	$23,951	$31,935	$39,918
Balance - 10 yrs.	$8,581	$17,162	$25,744	$34,325	$42,906
Total in 10 yrs.	$16,565	$33,130	$49,695	$66,259	$82,824

Saving $10,000 may not seem worth it, but if you invest in a 30 year note at 7%, you will have 79.8% of your money back ($7,984) in 10 years. The borrower will still owe you 85.8% of your original investment ($8,581) with 20 years left to pay. Over several vehicle purchases, you can reach $50,000 in savings, which adds $3,992 per year to your income. During the first 10 years you would receive $39,918 and still be owed $42,906. The 240 remaining payments of $332.65 pay *another* $79,836, bringing the total from your $50,000 investment to $119,754 over 30 years.

Figure 21-6 summarizes the note income you might receive by following suggestions in this book to convert assets that don't produce income into notes.

Figure 21-6 Potential Note Income Summary

Asset Description	Potential Note Amt.		Income / mo.		Income / yr.	
	Min.	Max.	Min.	Max.	Min.	Max.
HECM Loan	$74,200	$371,000	$494	$2,468	$5,924	$29,619
Car Savings	$10,000	$50,000	$67	$333	$798	$3,992
Lazy Money	$5,000	$35,000	$33	$233	$399	$2,794
Roth IRA	$8,000	$16,000	$53	$106	$639	$1,277
HSA	$4,150	$8,300	$28	$55	$331	$663
Total	$101,350	$480,300	$674	$3,195	$8,091	$38,345

Notes rarely last the full 30-year term. If the borrowers sell or refinance their property, your note will be paid off. If that happens, you simply fund another note with a new amortization schedule that resets the 30-year clock. The new payment will have more going toward interest and less toward principal than the seasoned note that was paid off.

22

Discover Your Destiny

"Do what you love and the money will follow."
— Marsha Sinetar

RETIREMENT HACKING

In 1943, Abraham Maslow, an American psychologist, published a paper titled, *A Theory of Human Motivation*. The theory is a classification of human needs that later became known as *Maslow's Hierarchy of Needs*. According to Maslow, after our physical needs of air, water, food and shelter, the next highest need is the need to be *needed*.

Many couples retire after their children are grown, educated, married, and on their own. If their self-sufficient children no longer need them, or at least as much, the parents' need to be needed is achieved through their grandchildren. This explains why grandparents and grandchildren get along so well - they have a common foe.

My mother got a pilot's license and owned her own airplane in 1956, but postponed her traveling ambitions for decades to care for my dad, five siblings and me. When my parent's retirement plans were cut short by my father's death in 1996, mom resumed traveling the world and acquired more than a dozen timeshare condominiums along the way.

Rather than being snowbound in North Dakota, she'd spend winters in Cabo San Lucas, Mexico. She traveled well into her 80s until her advanced age and cancer finally started to slow her down. During a visit with her near the end of her life, I suggested that maybe she should sell some of her timeshares as she wasn't able to use them as often as she once did. Mom retrieved a yellow legal pad bearing the names of the 22 families who'd enjoyed her condos the previous year. She said, "These are the families I sent on vacation last year and they'll remember it for the rest of their lives."

It was then that I realized that mom's timeshares were no longer for her enjoyment. They'd transitioned from being a warm, tropical alternative to spending her winters in North Dakota, to becoming a gift she could give to others. Sharing her condos satisfied her need to be needed. It became her *why*.

Finding condos for her friends and family gave mom a purpose. She'd spend days searching for available timeshare units that aligned with people's travel schedules. Enabling others to create family memories in the timeshares she had enjoyed for more than two decades gave her great pleasure.

I saw a similar phenomenon in my engineering job at Raytheon. Older engineers who'd reached the peak of their careers would get immense satisfaction from helping younger engineers climb higher on the corporate ladder than they'd been able to reach themselves.

After 22 years, I retired from Raytheon in 2002. I found my passion in real estate, helping people understand the market cycles, the benefits of owning rental properties, and the right time to buy and sell. After 22 years in my second career, we're now helping the *children* of our clients and friends create budgets, buy homes, and plan for retirement, but we've transitioned again, this time to note investing.

Many of the clients who purchased rental properties from us over the past two decades are retiring. I've found my new niche helping our friends and clients get note income from the same properties they've rented for decades, without the headaches, hassles, drama, or trauma of being a landlord.

At a family reunion in Colorado several years ago, the main topic of conversation with my siblings was when we'd retire, what we'd do, and where we'd live. My siblings now invest with me in a variety of secure real estate notes that provide predictable monthly payments to subsidize their pensions and Social Security.

My purpose has transitioned from my engineering job to educating clients about the real estate market to becoming a trusted advisor to friends and family members. I enjoy helping others create wealth and increase their income so they can enjoy a better lifestyle.

My wife and I have owned a motor home since 2002, but most of the miles driven were between Tucson, Arizona, and Houston, Texas, where her family lived. When I turned 60, we started taking longer trips. What started as deadhead trips to visit family over the holidays has turned into a month-long RV trip every quarter for us and our three dogs.

Through real estate coaching and national conferences, we have friends in nearly every major city in the United States and Canada. I schedule speaking engagements to teach as many people as possible how to fund notes that create passive income streams in addition to their job. It's a true *win-win-win* scenario. We get to explore the country and see friends we've known for decades, they receive additional income from notes they fund, while helping local business owners buy the homes that mainstream lenders told them they weren't qualified to purchase. Nobody loses except the banks that wouldn't give the business owners a loan.

Find something you like to do and are passionate about. I became involved with the Make-A-Wish Foundation in 2008 and have hosted a note conference every year since 2009 to share everything I've learned about real estate, finances, and life. People from all over the country attend and donate items to be auctioned off. Since 2009, our conference has raised $668,000 for Make-A-Wish. I'm two-thirds of the way to reaching the goal set on my 50th birthday - to give the Make-A-Wish Foundation one million dollars before I die.

In 2012, I published a book, *A Daily Difference*, to share how friends around the country have integrated charitable giving into their businesses. Since then, I've seen many others find their passion. My friend Tom Olson in Indiana founded a real estate investment company called *Good Success*. The company motto is "Be a conduit, not a bucket" and the mission statement is "Work, to have, to give." Tom and his wife, Becky, take what they need from their business and pass the rest on to help others.

Augie Byllott is another friend who's leaving the world better than he found it. Augie's passion is giving people the gift of mobility. As the chairman of *Chair the Love*, a Florida nonprofit, Augie and his wife, Audrey, raise money to provide wheelchairs for people who can't afford them. In 2023 alone, they filled 13 shipping containers with 280 wheelchairs each. They have delivered more than 10,000 wheelchairs to people in nine countries on four continents.

What is your purpose? What is your *why?* Being retired doesn't mean sitting around doing nothing. *Do something!*

23

Leaving a Legacy

"If your plan is for one year, plant rice; if your plan is for ten years, plant trees. If your plan is for one hundred years, educate children"
— *Confucius*

Benjamin Franklin is widely known for his famous quote, "A penny saved is a penny earned." Franklin was born in Boston, but moved to Philadelphia when he was 17 years old. He served as the Governor of Pennsylvania from 1785 to 1788, but had a firm belief that politicians in a democracy shouldn't be paid. When he died in 1790, Franklin bequeathed the salary (about $4,000 at the time) that he received as Governor to the cities of Boston and Philadelphia.

Franklin stipulated that the money left to each city be invested for 200 years and used to provide low-interest loans to married tradesmen under the age of 26 who wished to start a business. Franklin had started his printing business using a loan and wished to extend the favor to future generations. After the first 100 years, each city could spend 75% of the balance for public works projects and invest the remaining 25% for another 100 years. After 200 years, the trust account would end and the money could be spent as each city saw fit.

After the first one hundred years, the city of Philadelphia had grown their $4,000 to $70,000, but Boston's had ballooned to more than $327,000. With their 75% of the fund, Philadelphia created the Franklin Institute. Boston used their 75% to fund the Benjamin Franklin Institute of Technology in honor of Franklin's high regard for education. Even with allegations of corruption and misuse of the funds, by the end of the second hundred years, Philadelphia's trust had grown to $2,000,000 and Boston's fund grew to $4,500,000. It seems that a penny saved is *not* a penny earned; it's a penny that's multiplied by 1,625 over 200 years ($6,500,000 total / $4,000invested = 1,625).

We all have an expiration date. We've known it all our life and it becomes more evident with every grandparent, parent, uncle, aunt, sibling, and friend that passes away before us. The question to ask yourself is, "What's better because I was here?"

For most people, their legacy is their children, grandchildren, and future generations that will continue to be born long after they're gone. Aside from leaving them your money and belongings, what can you do to make their life better?

I believe that the best thing you can leave behind is your *wisdom*. As we've bumbled our way through life, we've all made mistakes, especially when we were younger. Whoever said, "Experience comes with scars" was right. You probably learned a lot by doing things wrong the first time, correcting your mistakes, and taking the new-found knowledge with you.

An amazing gift to share with your family would be all the things you did wrong. Making mistakes is how we learn, but what if your mistakes could help others avoid the pitfalls you encountered? Sharing your missteps could help your children and grandchildren avoid them in the first place. But what if you haven't corrected them?

The one thing nobody should die with is *regret*. Make a list of all the things you wanted to do but never accomplished in your life. It doesn't matter if it's a trip, experience, meal, or conversation. Make a "bucket list" of the things you want to do before you die. Going back to do the things you missed or messed up would be a great retirement!

I had some good visits with my mom toward the end of her life. I'd helped her manage her money for 25 years after my dad died. I told mom that I thought inheritance should skip a generation. My siblings and I were all in our 50s and 60s and nearing retirement. None of us needed her money, but her twelve grandchildren were aged 16 to 36 when she died. They were going to college, getting married, having children, and buying their first homes. They needed mom's money more than we did.

I convinced mom to open a Roth IRA when she was 82 years old. She'd lived comfortably for the 20 years since my father passed away, so she naturally asked, "Why do I need a Roth IRA?" I replied, "You *don't* need it; your grandchildren do." I explained that when she died, her grandchildren would inherit her *age,* and thus her ability to receive tax-free income for the rest of their lives without being 59½ years old. I told her, "The best way to keep your photo on the fireplace is to give your grandchildren tax-free income for the rest of their lives."

Mom took my advice and opened a Roth IRA with $6,000, which was $500 for each of her twelve grandchildren. Mom hadn't worked in 30 years and had no *earned* income to contribute to a Roth IRA, so she rolled over funds from a traditional IRA to fund the account. To grow the money quickly, I helped her partner with investor friends to fund short-term investments that paid a high rate of return.

While visiting with mom a few years later, she said "Bob, I keep getting these emails from *Questira* telling me that they've deposited money to my account. Is that a *scam?*"

I assured mom that the emails from Quest IRA (now Quest Trust Company) were legit, and proceeded to explain each of the investments she'd bought, sold, and currently held in her Roth IRA account. After realizing that her initial deposit had grown by more than 40%, mom rolled over another $36,000, six times more than her initial investment, from her Traditional IRA.

Mom passed away in September, 2019, just 54 days before the SECURE Act changed the rules for inherited Roth IRAs. On December 20, 2019, the length of time non-spouse beneficiaries can receive tax-free income from inherited Roth IRAs was reduced from their entire lifetime to 10 years. Mom's grandchildren received the lifetime benefit, but now anyone who inherits a Roth IRA must close the account after 10 years to stop the tax-free income.

By the time of her death, the Roth IRA account opened for her grandchildren owned seven real estate notes and had doubled in value. Thanks to a conversation I had with my friend, Quincy Long, founder and CEO of Quest Trust Company, mom changed the beneficiary election of her Roth IRA a few months before she died.

Instead of each grandchild receiving 1/12 of each note she owned, mom created a *trust* which inherited all of the assets in the Roth IRA and her grandchildren are the beneficiaries. If each note had been divided twelve ways, there would have been 84 assets to track. I calculated that, due to the small balance in each grandchild's inherited Roth IRA account, the investments would have to earn 21% to pay the custodial fees.

When mom died, none of the notes had to be divided; they all remained intact in the trust. How many company owners would give you advice that results in you paying them significantly less each year in fees? Quincy Long has impacted many people's lives by sharing his time and vast knowledge about retirement accounts, trusts, and the IRS tax code. I learned much of the information in this book from Quincy.

When she was alive, mom would give each of her grandchildren a crisp $100 bill for Christmas. The first distribution from her Roth IRA trust was almost 50% more than the Christmas gifts received when she was alive. Her annual gift will increase in value every year as the balance of the account increases and a higher percentage is distributed. Her twelve grandchildren will each receive more than *one hundred thousand dollars* from mom's $42,000 gift.

What can you do to make someone's life better?
Pay It Forward!

Bob Zachmeier

HOW TO FIND OUT MORE ABOUT NOTES

If you've enjoyed reading this book, please share it with others and go to: *www.amazon.com/Bob-Zachmeier/e/B0044P1EIY* to leave a favorable review.

If you'd like to purchase my software which enables you to structure seller-financed deals in your area in under a minute, go to: *www.NoteCarry.com.*

If you'd like more information about note investing or would like to test drive the weekly mentoring webinars I host for the NoteCarry Network, send an e-mail to *bob@notecarry.com.*

For information about my annual note-investing conference, go to *www.NoteBusinessBuilder.com* and get registered! If you'd like to purchase recordings from previous conferences, send an e-mail to *bob@notecarry.com.* Make-A-Wish Arizona receives 100% of the proceeds

If you'd like to access free resources to help you plan your own retirement, go to: *www.NoteCarry.com.* Many of the charts in this book can be modified with your specific information.

For information about books written by Bob Zachmeier, visit: *www.OutOfTheBoxBooks.com* or just send an e-mail to: *bob@notecarry.com.*

<u>ABOUT THE AUTHOR</u>

Bob Zachmeier was born and raised in Mandan, North Dakota. His parents taught by example that determination and a strong work ethic could achieve almost any goal. As the third of six children, Zachmeier learned to become self-reliant. He started a fireworks business at the age of 16 with billboard and radio advertising. The business helped to fund his college education and that of his siblings.

Zachmeier became a real estate agent in 2000 at the age of 40. By 2002, he was earning enough from real estate investments to leave his job and end a twenty-two-year career in the defense electronics industry. In 2004, Zachmeier and his wife, Camille, founded Win3 Realty in Tucson, Arizona. The name reflected their desire to create *win-win-win* situations for their clients, their company, and their community. They've raised over $668,000 for the Make-A-Wish Foundation and have received several philanthropic awards.

In 2023, Zachmeier observed that many retirees were having trouble paying their bills due to the highest inflation in 40 years. He began helping them get more of their assets producing income. Soon friends, family, and past clients were getting better returns than they earned at the bank without the volatility of the stock market. His website, ***www.NoteCarry.com*** offers hundreds of hours of training, and software tools that teach others how to help the buyers, sellers, and retirees in their community with real estate notes.

By sharing his experience and practical advice as a real estate broker, coach, college instructor, author, lecturer, and note investor, Bob Zachmeier has helped thousands of people improve their financial well-being. His books include: *Upside Up Real Estate Investing, Sold On Change!, Answers From Experts on Buying a Home, Answers From Experts on Selling a Home, A Daily Difference, Who Needs the Bank?* and *Retirement Hacking.*